50 CAMPAIGNS
TO SHOUT
ABOUT

Also by Ellie Levenson

The Noughtie Girl's Guide to Feminism

50 CAMPAIGNS
TO SHOUT
ABOUT

Ellie Levenson

ONEWORLD
OXFORD

A Oneworld Paperback Original

Published by Oneworld Publications 2011

ISBN 978-1-85168-771-8

Typeset by Jayvee, Trivandrum, India
Cover design by BoldandNoble.com
Printed and bound by CPI Cox & Wyman, Reading, RG1 8EX

Oneworld Publications
185 Banbury Road
Oxford OX2 7AR
England

Learn more about Oneworld. Join our mailing list to
find out about our latest titles and special offers at:

www.oneworld-publications.com

Contents

Introduction:
Get some issues

Our lives begin to end the day we become silent
about things that matter
Martin Luther King Jr.

It's easy, when watching the news, reading the paper, or just getting on with life and absorbing bits of information about the world, to assume that bad things happen, well, just because life is sometimes unfair, and that unless you have a massive idea and an equally massive amount of money to support you, then there's little you can do about it. But there are many areas in our lives where individuals and groups of individuals can change things, helping to make the world kinder, cleaner, or fairer. From encouraging shops to stock ethical goods to standing up and denouncing racism or homophobia, from asking your elected representative to lobby government on your behalf to doing a spot of guerrilla gardening, we all have the ability to try to make our community, or even the world, a better place.

This book is about getting involved and making a difference. Some people shy away from both of these things; getting involved is seen as being too much like a busybody, and making a difference is seen as impossible. Without wishing to sound like a schmaltzy self-help book, these are just barriers, or excuses. There are loads of small things we can do in our day-to-day lives that make a difference to the issues that we each care deeply about, and some big things we can do too. Whatever it is you care about – and I bet there are many things that irk you every day, whether it's dog poo on the pavement outside your house, the unfairness of a system that allows bankers to earn millions while the people who clean their offices don't earn a 'living wage', or the thousands who die each day due to a lack of clean water or healthcare – nearly every issue or campaign allows us the opening to do just as much as we feel able to do.

This book identifies fifty such issues or campaigns that offer the opportunity for changing things if enough people take the step to do so.

◆

In the 1940s, the UK government commissioned William Beveridge, an economist and campaigner, to study the social challenges facing the country. The Beveridge Report identified five 'giants' that brought shame to our society: squalor, ignorance, want, idleness, and disease. The report proposed massive reforms to the British system of social welfare which formed the basis of the modern welfare state, including the National Health Service.

Squalor, ignorance, want, idleness, and disease all still exist, and many of the campaigns put forward in this book fit into these categories. But society's modern ills fit into other categories, too. If I were to choose the 'giants' plaguing us today they might include Beveridge's five as well as unfairness, lack of compassion, the environment, and a category I can only think to call 'civilization' – the idea that a particular ethical or legal situation demeans everyone, such as the existence of a death penalty or the lack of representation for women in a nation's structures of power.

Categorizing issues is difficult, though. One of the campaigns in this book is 'Be kind to refugees and migrants'. 'Kind' is an admittedly fluffy word, here encompassing the idea of looking after people who, having left their own country, have arrived in yours with very little; it involves empathy, a need to imagine the insecurity, isolation, and vulnerability these refugees and migrants might feel. They need homes and money and education and jobs, but they also need other people to reach out to them with a feeling of welcome and warmth – almost the opposite of what many refugees and migrants currently experience on their arrival. How do you label these sorts of things? Is a campaign on behalf of refugees and migrants about poverty, ignorance, and want? Is it about racial justice, compassion, fairness, and civilization? Or is it about some combination of all of these challenges and aspirations? The boundaries blur.

This book is full of similarly 'fluffy' and 'soft' phrases: 'be nice', 'be kind', 'empathize'. I make no apology for that; the world is a better, nicer place when we are, well, nice. When you come to think of it, every campaign I've included could easily fall under the banner of 'be nice' or 'be responsible'. That's what making a difference is about.

It is reasonable, however, to agree that we should be nice to one another and yet to still ask what difference one's actions can actually make to a campaign. It's true that sometimes, to really take off, a cause has to capture the public imagination on a large scale. Some years ago, when I was working for the UK-based charity End Child Poverty, I was chatting with a senior editor on a national tabloid newspaper. He said he would put our cause on the paper's front page, even highlight every one of the specific policy changes we were advocating for adoption by the government in Westminster, if I could get him photographs of Victoria and David Beckham – or someone equally famous – holding a tea party for poor British children. But End Child Poverty didn't have celebrity ambassadors, and I seemed to have forgotten to put the Beckhams in my address book. Unless you are working for a charity with a host of celebrities at its disposal, or happen to have a well-known person in the family or living next door, you're unlikely to be able to pull together this kind of photo opportunity either.

But numerous campaigns have proved that you don't need to hold celebrity tea parties to make a difference. Sometimes change can be achieved by getting enough people to write to their MP, by refusing to shop in certain stores, or by working out how to frame an idea – such as the realization amongst the campaigners for a workplace smoking ban in the UK that their campaign would be more successful if it was framed as a workers' rights issue rather than as a health one.

For some campaigns the most effective thing you can do is get involved personally. Not all of us have the time or inclination to be full-time campaigners, either as a job or in an unpaid capacity, but we can make campaigning part of our everyday lives. Take the campaign to limit the amount of plastic bags and packaging we use. You can do something as small as buy a reusable bag, or you can take the time and effort to send excess packaging back to the companies who use it. Or you can, to take another example, become a school governor. Though it may not be as quick and easy as buying a reusable bag, serving as a governor puts you in a position where you can help write the anti-bullying policy for your local school, ensuring it takes homophobic bullying just as seriously as other types of bullying. Taking action like this won't feel small to you, or to the people being bullied. But it's the sort of change that happens person by person, since it's not as though bullying is going to make it onto the legislative agenda, and it's easy enough for bullies to dismiss a distant celebrity, whom they'll never know, speaking up in an ad campaign.

For other campaigns the actions might seem a little odd at first. To help prevent human trafficking, one of the best things you can do is, if you visit a sex worker, to ask whether he or she is there willingly. This does not mean I am necessarily condoning the use of prostitutes or other sex workers, but it does mean that if you are going to use their services, then you should at the same time ensure you are not participating in the modern-day equivalent of slavery.

It's a common mistake to assume that if you are a campaigner you must also be party political, especially if one or other political party agrees with you on a particular issue. But this book is not about party politics, it's about the issues that affect us all, whatever our ideology and our voting preferences. One of the motivations of campaigning around issues rather than party manifestos is that issues can unite people in a way that party politics do not. No matter how our solutions differ, we can all want to ensure that the elderly are not abandoned to financial and emotional poverty or that preventable diseases are actually prevented. And sometimes one of the most inspirational things about getting involved is finding other people, from a variety of backgrounds and with a variety of opinions, who share your passion for a cause. So something as simple as making your community a safer, friendlier, greener – that is, nicer – place to live can get you thinking about joining up on other campaigns, too.

◆

There are far more than fifty issues to be addressed in the world, of course, and if you sat down and came up with a list of fifty issues it's quite unlikely it would be exactly the same as my list. But I hope that reading this book will not only inspire you to get involved in the campaigns I have highlighted but will also inspire you to have a think about other things you care about and how you can change these, too.

One thing you are likely to notice is that climate change doesn't make it into my fifty, though it does sneak a mention as no. 51 at the end of this book, where my suggestion is to go online and check out a number of organizations' websites. Why? The problem is that climate change is a huge issue, one that requires change on a world-wide level, involving national governments and global businesses. This book could be filled with fifty campaigns dedicated solely to climate change – and there are other books that do just that. So I decided to include some environmental causes that deal with our health, our oversized consumption patterns, and the conservation of natural places so that everyone in society will be able to enjoy them, and leave a proper exploration of what we can do about climate change to others. But it's most definitely a campaign you need to shout about, so I didn't want to leave it out completely.

Throughout the book, I've included case studies of successful campaigns and tips from seasoned campaigners, covering practical ideas for everything from how to organize an event to how to motivate volunteers, from how to write an effective letter to an elected representative to how to raise money for a cause, and from how to make the most of the internet to how to obtain press interest in your activities. Experts include Baroness Hollis, who stresses the importance of showing how an issue affects real lives, which was a tactic she used to campaign successfully for better pension provision for women, and Adrian Lovett, from the Jubilee 2000 campaign to Drop the Debt, who explains how personal letters to decision makers have a real influence, especially if one is sent to the Chancellor of the Exchequer by his own mum!

At the heart of the book, however, are the fifty campaigns. For each campaign or issue, you'll get a 'call to action' – the reason this issue is important today and how it fits into our lives. You'll also find 'take action' points – suggestions for what you can do to make a difference, be it today, tomorrow, next month, or next year. These include things you can do as an individual, with your friends, with your school, or with your employer, and range from learning to cook with leftovers so you don't waste food to researching the planning applications being considered by your local council and making a decision to support or object to them. The actions suggested for each campaign are just to start you off. If an issue touches on your life or your local area then you become an expert yourself; any personal knowledge you bring to a campaign will give you the passion you need to help change other people's minds about it.

Which brings me to my last point. What this book isn't meant to be is a holier-than-thou sanctimonious handbook. Though I chose all the campaigns in this book because I believe they are important, I certainly haven't dedicated myself to all of them, let alone adopted every action point I've suggested. Indeed, I can be a terrible hypocrite when it comes to some of these issues: I leave lights on, throw food away, use plastic bags, ignore petitions, never attend my local council's meetings, and fail to do dozens of things every day that could make our lives nicer. But I do try to do some of them, some of the time. Since starting to write this book I have become a school governor, enlisted as an e-mentor for a sixth former, and signed up to a prisoner pen-friend scheme. Not surprisingly, all three of these actions involve education and writing, two subjects that particularly interest me. But that is the point of getting involved with issue-based campaigning – you can do precisely what interests you, at precisely the level you want.

A note on contact information

All contact information for organizations was correct at the time this book went to press. But websites change and organizations move, close, and merge, so apologies in advance if any of the information listed is out of date.

Luckily, with easy access to information on the internet, it should be relatively easy to find people and organizations with the same aims and ideals as you, and to share ideas about making a difference.

However, when doing this search, it may be hard to work out which organizations are legitimate or who their backers are. There are no hard and fast rules for assessing non-governmental organizations (NGOs), but there are some guidelines you can follow.

In the UK all charities with an income over a certain level (£5000 at the time of going to press) and with its head office in the UK must register with the Charity Commission (for England and Wales) or its Scottish or Northern Irish counterparts. If you are concerned about whether a charity is real then you can check it on their register at www.charity-commission.gov.uk.

Not all campaigning organizations are charities. But there are often other clues you can look for to check out whether you should trust the organization. Does its website list an address and phone number and do these work? Is it clear who the staff members and founders are? Is the website kept up to date? Does it list the sources of its information? If you are in any doubt over the legitimacy of an organization, do not give it your contact details or any money.

1

Provide a home for everyone

At its worst, homelessness entails sleeping on the streets. In London alone, 3500 people sleep on the streets at some point each year – 250 people on any one night. Shockingly, according to the charity Crisis, such 'rough sleepers' have a life expectancy of just forty-two years.

But homelessness encompasses more than these potentially dangerous and soul-destroying situations. It includes living in squats, which in many cases lack electricity or running water, and which involves breaking the law and risking arrest. It also includes living in a B&B or other temporary accommodation, which, if they're affordable, are often of a low standard, and which can cause people to feel a lack of control. Homelessness even includes living in overcrowded flats with family or friends, in what is known as 'concealed housing' – that is, sleeping on the floor or a sofa, when the space is available.

The limbo of homelessness is dislocating and isolating. As well as not having the comfort of a space to call home, the lack of a permanent address can make it difficult, even impossible, to get a permanent job, receive benefits, get paid for work, build a history of credit, or stay in touch with loved ones. What's more, homeless people have high levels of other vulnerabilities, including mental health problems, drug and alcohol dependencies, abuse, and other traumatic experiences, and these become exacerbated without proper help and support.

Think about how much it means to you to have a physical space you can call 'home', a place where you can go at the end of a day and know you will be warm and safe. It might be big or it might be small, but it is a space where you can relax, be yourself, and keep your possessions. Such a place is something everyone deserves.

Take Action

▶ *Give in kind.* Persuade your employer or a local business to donate 'in kind', which means to donate things rather than money. For example, homelessness charities are often looking for paints and brushes to stock their art room. Are there any lying about in that recently renovated café on the high street that could be given away? IT equipment is often needed for job training and administration. Has your company recently upgraded its computers or changed its routers? Or while you're cleaning out your own home you may find second-hand bikes or bike parts that could be used in a homelessness centre's bicycle repair workshops, or musical instruments that might provide a creative outlet for homeless children and families.

▶ *Ask for better housing.* Help prevent people becoming homeless in the first place. Monitor the planning applications for 'new build' developments filed with your local council – these will be available to view online – and if you see an application that includes affordable housing, send a letter of support. Attend the local council meeting and use the public questions time to request that more affordable homes be built in your area. And find out which of your council members is in charge of housing, and write to him or her to ask the same.

▶ *Make the homeless visible.* Keep an eye out for rough sleepers as you walk around your neighbourhood or make your commute to work. If you are concerned about the safety or health of a rough sleeper, let a local homelessness charity know. Its outreach team can try to make contact with the person and see if he or she needs assistance of any kind.

*The ache for home lives in all of us, the safe place
where we can go as we are and not be questioned*

MAYA ANGELOU

Where to Get Started

Shelter works to alleviate the distress caused by homelessness and bad housing.
88 Old Street
London EC1V 9HU
Tel 0844 515 2000
www.shelter.org.uk

Crisis provides resources for single people who are homeless across the UK.
66 Commercial Street
London E1 6LT
Tel 084 4251 0111
www.crisis.org.uk

St Mungo's is a London-based charity providing accommodation, support projects, and emergency services to homeless people and working to prevent homelessness.
St Mungo's Griffin House
161 Hammersmith Road
London W6 8BS
Tel 020 8762 5500
www.mungos.org

On the ground:
Get to know the people you're helping

Jessica Studdert previously worked for St Mungo's, the charity working with London's homeless (www.mungos.org). She stresses the importance of finding out what the people you're helping want and including them in the campaign.

Q *Tell me about your campaign on mental health and homelessness.*

A At St Mungo's we devised a campaign to raise awareness of mental health problems amongst street homeless people and campaign for better services for them. There was a clear gap in the health services available, especially for people who end up on the streets. Street homelessness is often caused and prolonged by a health problem, and mental health problems are the most under-resourced area of the NHS.

Because we were emphasizing that this was a health issue, not a housing issue, we wanted the Department of Health, rather than the Department of Communities and Local Government, to address the problem. We also wanted to make sure that our goals and our key campaign messages matched the reality of life on the streets for homeless people, not our assumptions as charity professionals.

Q *How did you go about getting information from homeless people about what they needed and wanted to improve their health?*

A The first thing we did was gather a group of currently home-less people for a two-day discussion session. The idea was to gen-erate a set of questions that they would take out to the streets. They would ask other homeless people about their individual experiences and bring that substantive information back to us, so we could incorporate it into the campaign's goals and messages.

Because homeless people often distrust authority figures and professionals, who have frequently let them down in the past, this 'peer research' approach works much better. They are much more likely to open up to someone who has 'been there' than to a pro-fessional 'busybody'. The homeless people who had volunteered for our discussion session were able to interview one hundred other homeless people – including fifteen or so who were cur-rently on the streets and completely disengaged from society. The information they gathered was gold; they were giving voice to a group of people who are usually voiceless, and making their expe-riences central to our campaign for health services.

Q *How did you use the information that was gathered by the peer researcher team?*

A On the basis that the real Health Select Committee wouldn't take up mental health services for the homeless as an issue, we held a mock committee event at Parliament. As part of the event, we hosted a reception at which one of the peer researchers spoke. He had the guests gripped as he described his own spiral into drug addiction after the death of his daughter – he hadn't received the support he needed during his grief and, unable to get access to pro-fessional mental health services, he had ended up on the streets.

At the same time we launched a national 'Call for Evidence on Mental Health and Street Homelessness'. This was run on the model of a government consultation because we wanted to make the point that the Department of Health wouldn't do their own consultation to solicit the opinion of experts in this area. We got eighty responses from professionals, the voluntary sector, and government departments, from which we published a major report outlining clear actions for the government to take.

So much of the campaign involved getting in front of the government the voices of people who usually don't get to speak directly to the government. But we also used the voices of St Mungo's donors and supporters – we got them to write to their members in Parliament, using a template letter, to ask that the minister for mental health consider the mental health needs of homeless people. This public involvement added to the momentum we had on the issue.

In the end, the Department of Health's next mental health strategy contained explicit reference to street homelessness, something they had never previously recognized responsibility for.

2

Support our military

It sometimes seems fashionable to view the military as either unwitting stooges used by corrupt governments or as returning, triumphant heroes. In fact most members of the military are neither of these. They are ordinary people who work as public servants in extraordinary circumstances, carrying out the decisions made by our government. Few of us would like there to be no military at all: they help to maintain our feeling of security every day and respond to disasters at home and abroad. Even people who are opposed to all offensive military actions can appreciate the huge amount of peacekeeping and humanitarian work carried out by the military.

Members of our armed forces work exceptionally hard and frequently put their lives in danger. They earn a relatively low wage, are required to work very long hours, and leave their families behind for long stretches of time. Yet we often fail them when they return to civilian life. High numbers end up in prison or homeless, or find it hard to get a civilian job. A 2009 article in the *Guardian* reported a study by Napo, the family court and probation officers' trade union, which showed that 20,000 former servicemen were in prison or on probation or parole in the UK – over double the number of British servicemen serving in Afghanistan at the time. Of these former military personnel, 8500 were in prison – almost one in ten of the full prison population. The study also found evidence linking mental health problems, alcohol and drug abuse, and domestic violence with the experience of serving in combat zones.

How we view our military and ex-military often comes down to our views of a particular political situation. But whatever you think about a specific conflict and whatever preconceptions you may have about military life, we owe it to these men and women to make life for them and their dependents easier, not harder.

Never in the field of human conflict was so much owed by so many to so few

WINSTON CHURCHILL DURING THE BATTLE OF BRITAIN, 20 AUGUST 1940

Take Action

▶ *Show your support.* The Poppy Appeal is one of the Royal British Legion's biggest fundraising and awareness-raising activities. Red paper poppies are worn in the UK in the run up to Remembrance Day, held each year on 11 November, to commemorate members of the armed services who have died. You can volunteer to help the Royal British Legion sell poppies, or just buy one to wear as a show of your support. In the USA, 'Buddy Poppies' are sold by the Veterans of Foreign Wars around Veteran's Day, which is also observed on 11 November, with the last Monday in May, Memorial Day, dedicated to remembering those who gave their lives in conflict.

▶ *Give your time.* Consider volunteering for the Royal British Legion or another charity as a case worker or visitor to a military veteran or surviving family member. Roles include giving former military members advice on compensation entitlements and state benefits, providing support through bereavement or other family crises, and visiting ex-service men and women who are housebound or in hospital.

Where to Get Started

The **Royal British Legion** safeguards the welfare, interests, and memory of those who are serving or who have served in the armed forces.
199 Borough High Street
London SE1 1AA
Tel 020 3207 2100
www.britishlegion.co.uk

Help for Heroes raises money to provide services to members of the military who have been wounded in Iraq and Afghanistan.
Unit 6, Aspire Business Centre
Ordnance Road
Tidworth
Hampshire SP9 7QD
Tel 0845 673 1760
www.helpforheroes.org.uk

Veterans of Foreign Wars of the United States is the largest US organization of combat veterans. It campaigns on veterans' rights and promotes community service.
406 West 34th Street
Kansas City, MO 64111
USA
Tel +1 816 756 3390
www.vfw.org

3

Look after your local community

The 'broken windows' theory says that if some things in a community are left broken or dirty then the community declines, both physically and socially, as people come to believe that vandalism, littering, and other anti-social behaviour is tolerated or even accepted.

So, when it comes to litter, you are less likely to drop your own litter if the street is clean than if it is already strewn with other people's rubbish. Similarly, an experiment at the University of Groningen, in the Netherlands, found that when an envelope with a clearly visible five-euro note was placed into three different mailboxes in the same area – one a clean mailbox, one a graffiti-covered mailbox, and one a mailbox with litter surrounding it, the incidences of a passer-by stealing the money doubled when the mailbox suffered from graffiti or litter.

Following the thinking behind the broken windows theory, if you do something to make your local community nice, this inspires others to do the same – and makes your community nicer, too. Even small steps, such as planting some flowers or campaigning against dog poo, can change the environment dramatically by encouraging others to do the same. And if an area is clean and feels safe, then people are likely to make use of public spaces, in turn creating an environment that serves the community and becomes a place for socializing and recreation for all residents.

Take Action

▶ *Do some 'guerrilla gardening'.* Plant some bulbs or sprinkle some seeds in scrubland or neglected public areas. For tips on how to become a guerrilla gardener, or to see if a group is active in your area, visit the Guerrilla Gardening website (www.guerrillagardening.org). The most active groups on the site are located in Australia, Canada, France, Germany, Ireland, the Netherlands, Spain, the UK, and the USA.

▶ *Organize a neighbourhood clean up.* Get a group together to pick up litter and report any fly tipping or dumping to your local council.

▶ *Win the lottery.* There are lots of small grants and pots of money available for community schemes to use to make a difference to their local area, from creating a playground to starting a youth club. Your local library may have the applications forms and details of grants, or subscriptions to databases of grant-giving trusts. Your local council may also have money available for supporting community schemes.

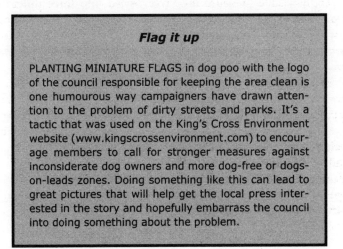

Flag it up

PLANTING MINIATURE FLAGS in dog poo with the logo of the council responsible for keeping the area clean is one humourous way campaigners have drawn attention to the problem of dirty streets and parks. It's a tactic that was used on the King's Cross Environment website (www.kingscrossenvironment.com) to encourage members to call for stronger measures against inconsiderate dog owners and more dog-free or dogs-on-leads zones. Doing something like this can lead to great pictures that will help get the local press interested in the story and hopefully embarrass the council into doing something about the problem.

▶ *Get to know your neighbours.* Arrange a seed and plant exchange where people in the community can offer or get advice on cultivating a garden. Or hold a 'skills swap shop' where they can exchange knowledge or services such as baking a birthday cake in return for their windows being cleaned or mowing the lawn in return for a lift to the shops.

▶ *Start a local paper – online.* Set up a website to share information about your community, or if one already exists find out how you can contribute to it. Talk About Local (see below) provides support for people interested in setting up a community website. These sites can cover anything of interest to the people in the community, including helpful notices about which dentists are open at weekends or which areas are unsafe to walk in alone or at night.

Where to Get Started

Talk About Local helps local communities organize online.
Studio 16, Fazeley Studios
191 Fazeley Street
Digbeth
Birmingham B5 5SE
Tel 0121 288 2910
www.talkaboutlocal.org.uk

Down to basics:
Online organizing

William Perrin is a community activist and the founder of Talk About Local (talkaboutlocal.org.uk). Since its launch in the summer of 2009, Talk About Local has provided technical support and suggestions to people who are looking to find their voice online in places ranging from Doddington, a village in Cambridgeshire, whose site includes a section listing the Parish Council Minutes, to the London postcode W14 (West Kensington), whose site includes blogs from residents and local business and event listings. Talk About Local is part of a larger movement towards 'hyperlocal' websites, sites that serve as an electronic equivalent of the town cryer, local public house, and neighbourhood association, all wrapped up in one, for a village, town, even a street or apartment block – the idea being that they help to give people a voice to communicate and campaign effectively in the places they live, work, and play.

Q *What is the first step to setting up a campaign online?*

A To get started, find one core place online where you will be able to keep all your reference material. As your campaign grows, other people online will want to link back to you – and you need a stable URL (better known as one of those web addresses that begin 'http://') that won't disappear. You can sign up as a user on Facebook and start a group page on the site, which allows you to invite other people to be administrators of the page, too. Or you can set up a simple blog, made using an internet-based service such as Wordpress.com or Blogger.com, both of which offer some design templates and storage options at no cost.

Q *What sorts of information are most effective online?*

A Photos, videos, and audio are a must – a picture, as they say, is worth a thousand words, and a genuinely angry, passionate person in a YouTube video is worth millions of them. Video can provide excellent evidence for getting your campaign attention – and getting it resolved. So find a digital camera or audio recorder, or a phone with good picture and sound quality, and use it as much as you can.

Q *How do I get other people involved?*

A Your online network of friends is a campaign waiting to happen. Use (but don't abuse) these people to get your campaign off the ground and spread the word.

But don't forget that campaigning existed long before the internet did. Talk to people who have run campaigns. Your parents or grandparents might have marched against the bomb or protested against the poll tax. They might not necessarily be online, but they can be very helpful in talking about the emotions that inspire people to join a campaign. Then convey those emotions on your Facebook page or website. An impassioned status update or blog post will make a difference.

Q *So why campaign online rather than take to the streets like previous generations did?*

A Geography isn't always important. If you are a customer of a company whose policies you are campaigning against, you are in a stronger position if you can get lots of other people to gang up and make a noise publicly. For that matter, companies and the government are not good at handling online campaigns. They tend to be slow in making public responses, so it is possible to run rings around them by using quick, everyday tools. YouTube, social networking site Facebook, and Foursquare (which lets you tap into and add to a list of local resources) all can handle uploads from mobile phones, to get information to the public within minutes of things happening. The democracy organization MySociety runs two websites – Write To Them (www.writetothem.com) and They Work for You (www.theyworkforyou.com) – that make it easy to be in touch with your elected representatives at all levels of government and to see what they are getting up to.

Q *Anything else I should bear in mind when using the internet and other new technology for campaigning?*

A You have to decide if you want to be fashionable or be effective – so choose your technology depending on whom you want to reach. The newer the technology, the fewer people you will reach. The biggest and best sites out there that help people are generally old-fashioned discussion forums – such as Sheffield's www.sheffieldforum.co.uk, which has 100,000 members in a city of 450,000 people. It's no use writing an iPhone app and expecting to reach a deprived neighbourhood. Remember that Barack Obama got elected mainly on email.

Also, when you put something online, you publish it online, so stay legal – if you say untrue things about people you can end up in big trouble.

And finally, newspapers and traditional journalists can help get your campaign noticed, but they also take control of what they write about your campaign and your website – and you might not agree with them. Request that any article links directly to your site so that people can see your argument in your own words and pictures.

♦

For more great tips on setting up your community website, from under-standing copyright and finding free images that will liven up your blog to creating links, maps, categories, groups, and many other online enhancements, visit Talk About Local's Step by Step Guides, which are available on their website. Their Quick Tips also offer ideas for what a community-based site might do, including posting stories about unsafe roads and junctions or highlighting how to get involved with a community garden or allotment.

The new website builder's glossary

WWW: usually added at the beginning of web addresses and stands for the world wide web, which was invented in 1990.

BROWSER: the software used to read web pages. Internet Explorer is commonly installed on computers; alternatives include Firefox, Chrome, and Opera.

URL: stands for 'uniform resource locator', this is a synonym for the address of a web page.

HTTP://: stands for 'hypertext transfer protocol', the means by which the web works. All URLs begin with this, but most browser software will automatically add this string of characters for you.

EMAIL: electronic mail, the equivalent to a postal address on the internet. Although you may not need to send or receive emails to use many common websites, an email account is required to sign up to most of them. Free providers include Googlemail, Hotmail, and Yahoo, and you can also set up email accounts through *Myguide* and many broadband hosts.

BLOG: short for weblog. Although the format generally includes a diary, the weblog is a very flexible way of publishing any sort of website without needing to use code or understand web hosting.

LINK/HYPERLINK: a portion of text on a web page that, when clicked, takes you to another page. It often looks slightly different to stand out from the rest of the text and is commonly underlined in blue. Some software allows you to highlight text and attach a hyperlink to it. On sites that allow simple hypertext markup, you can turn text into a hyperlink by typing: <a href ="[web page address, starting with http://]">[the text you want to be a link]</a>.

SOCIAL MEDIA/WEB 2.0: phrases fashionable at different times to denote websites that allow people to interact, for example blogs and social networks such as Facebook and Twitter. They are considered to be a phase further on from the first pages on the world wide web, which were normally static and didn't allow people to add their own words. On the other hand, email and internet message forums have been around much longer than 'web 2.0' websites and these also enable interaction. As do postcards and noticeboards ...

EMBED: blogs commonly allow you to include other types of content such as videos and photographs and this is usually referred to as 'embedding'. Sometimes problems can occur if you try to embed items that include different types of code than your webhost will allow, so check what your webhost requires if you plan to use a lot of photos, videos, or audio files.

TAG: an online indexing tool that allows you to search all of the content on a website for common terms, such as place names, people's names, or common nouns – actually, any combination of characters. Good tagging makes your posts more findable, which can lead to more viewers or readers, and perhaps introduce people in your area to your site. You can also use tags to gather together lots of people's photos or videos of an event by creating a unique tag and linking to it.

FEED/RSS FEED: Most websites are built using databases, which means their content can be pulled out and viewed in different ways. Feeds normally refer to lists of the most recent content added, and can be accessed in email, on a web page, or through RSS reader software.

WIDGET: pre-programmed mini applications that can be added into web browsers, WordPress and other websites, or a computer's desktop. Useful ones let you include other site feeds on your page, including Twitter posts, email subscription boxes, and photos uploaded to a photo-hosting website.

Source: Clare White, Talk About Local. Adapted and reprinted with permission.

4

Help prevent loneliness

Loneliness is more than teenagers who feels no one understands them, adults wishing they had a soul mate, or older people wanting to see more of their family. Loneliness is the condition in which a person may go for days without any human contact, for whom a transaction at the supermarket is the closest he or she gets to a conversation. And of course it is entirely possible to be surrounded by people and still feel an acute sense of loneliness. When any person is lonely, there's a great cost – to the person's own emotional and physical health and to the fabric of society.

In the UK, half a million pensioners are thought to have spent Christmas Day 2009 alone. According to University of Chicago neuroscientist John Cacioppo, the author of *Loneliness: Human Nature and the Need for Social Connection*, one in five people in America – that's 60 million people – feel so isolated that it makes them seriously unhappy. And a study cited in 'The Lonely Society?', a 2010 report on loneliness by the Mental Health Foundation, showed a link between loneliness and our physical health: women with breast cancer are four times more likely to die if they have no close friends than if they have ten friends or more.

It's not just elderly people who are lonely, as revealed by case studies collected by the Mental Health Foundation. Humans are social animals and to be without any human contact in solitary confinement is used as punishment and as a method of torture. Any decent society has an obligation to ensure that people do not suffer in their everyday lives, and that any person who craves friendship and conversation gets it.

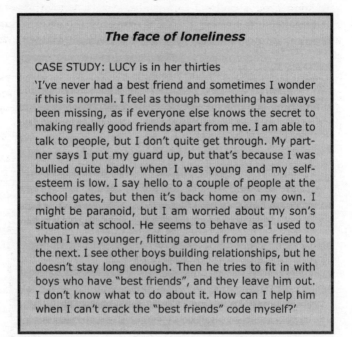

The face of loneliness

CASE STUDY: LUCY is in her thirties

'I've never had a best friend and sometimes I wonder if this is normal. I feel as though something has always been missing, as if everyone else knows the secret to making really good friends apart from me. I am able to talk to people, but I don't quite get through. My partner says I put my guard up, but that's because I was bullied quite badly when I was young and my self-esteem is low. I say hello to a couple of people at the school gates, but then it's back home on my own. I might be paranoid, but I am worried about my son's situation at school. He seems to behave as I used to when I was younger, flitting around from one friend to the next. I see other boys building relationships, but he doesn't stay long enough. Then he tries to fit in with boys who have "best friends", and they leave him out. I don't know what to do about it. How can I help him when I can't crack the "best friends" code myself?'

Take Action

▶ *Adopt a grandparent*. France, Italy, and the USA have adopt-a-granny schemes through which individuals or families can build up a relationship with an elderly person. Suggested activities include going for walks and inviting the person to a family dinner. And there's no reason to limit yourself to a grandparent or a formal volunteer programme: if you know someone who is far from family or who doesn't have one, invite him or her to dinner as an honorary aunt, uncle, brother, sister, parent, or, most simply, friend.

▶ *Create a community.* Encourage people of all ages and backgrounds to get involved with events in your community, such as gardening groups or local campaigns. And if you arrange an event, make sure you target invitations and activities for those who are often neglected, including the elderly, people with disabilities, and those in caring roles.

▶ *Lend a ride or a hand.* If you have a car, volunteer to help transport people to social events, especially the elderly or people with disabilities. Worries over transport can be one of the main reasons people don't get out and about. If you don't have a car, make an effort to say hello to neighbours who you believe have trouble getting out. Ask if they need anything from the shops, or help with an errand. Whether or not they take you up on your offer, you'll spend some time chatting.

The face of loneliness

CASE STUDY: MARTIN, age fifty-three

'I've lived on my own for twelve years now. I don't see it as a lifestyle choice: it's more something that just happened to me, and it's become a habit. I can see the benefits of living with other people and I do feel that I am missing something, that emotional comfort blanket that you have when you share a home. Sometimes I feel that my personality must be lacking something because I haven't managed to achieve that. I couldn't imagine living in a family set-up any more, but maybe in a community. I used to live in communal houses and I liked that feeling of all sitting down to eat together because I am quite domesticated and enjoy cooking for others. I probably would worry about being lonely later if my siblings didn't live nearby. What I'd like is if the area became more community orientated; if you could walk outside and meet people without worrying about being run over or mugged on the way to the shops.'

Where to Get Started

Mind is a charity working to promote and protect mental health. Its services include an information line for the public.
15–19 Broadway
London E15 4BQ
Tel 0845 766 0163
www.mind.org.uk

Age UK is a charity formed from the merger of Age Concern and Help the Aged. They conduct research, campaign, and run services around issues affecting people in later life.
York House
207–221 Pentonville Road
London N1 9UZ
Tel 0800 107 8977
www.ageuk.org.uk

Contact the Elderly organizes monthly Sunday afternoon tea parties for people over seventy-five who live alone with little or no support from family and friends.
15 Henrietta Street
Covent Garden
London WC2E 8QG
Tel 020 7240 0630
www.contact-the-elderly.org.uk

The face of loneliness

CASE STUDY: BERYL, age seventy-eight
'I am naturally sociable but lately I've been feeling isolated because of health problems. I couldn't walk for more than two years. It was very hard for me as I'd been used to meeting everyone out and about every day. I used to do the shopping and talk to the girls in the supermarket. For a while I got very down because I felt so cut off, and I was on anti-depressants for about six months. I thought I'd never walk again and I'd be stuck here in the house, staring at the same four walls. Now I am finally starting to walk again, I feel better. I can imagine getting back to my old ways.'

All case studies reprinted with permission from 'The Lonely Society?', a report of the Mental Health Foundation.

The **Mental Health Foundation** carries out research, campaigns, and works to improve services for anyone affected by mental health problems.
9th Floor, Sea Containers House
20 Upper Ground
London SE1 9QB
Tel 020 7803 1100
www.mentalhealth.org.uk

Little Brothers (Petits Frères) is an international befriending service operating in many countries, including France, where it was founded, and the USA.
64, avenue Parmentier
75011 Paris
France
Tel +33 (1) 4700 7968
www.petitsfreres.org
28 East Jackson Boulevard, Suite 405
Chicago, IL 60604–2263
USA
Tel +1 312 829 3055
www.littlebrothers.org

5

Support a free press

Freedom of the press is about more than being able to say what you want, when you want, a sort of glorified freedom of speech for people who work in the media. Freedom of the press is an essential part of democracy. It keeps a check on the people in power by asking them questions on behalf of the rest of us, and provides us with the information we need to make decisions on who to vote for, how to spend our money, and how to live safe and healthy lives.

To uncover and publish true versions of events, journalists need to be able to ask questions and write stories without obstruction, fear, or censorship. In a country like the UK or the USA, this means no injunctions 'gagging' the press from reporting on the government and particularly no 'super injunctions' that prevent them from even mentioning the existence of a court order stopping them from reporting something.

In some other countries it means putting an end to the practice of censoring what can and cannot be published in state-owned and even privately owned media outlets, or of imprisoning, harassing, or even killing journalists for doing their jobs – such as in the case of the Russian journalist Anna Politkovskaya, special correspondent for *Novaya Gazeta*. Politkovskaya was a fierce critic of the Kremlin who gained international recognition investigating human rights abuses, including in her 2001 book *A Dirty War: A Russian Reporter in Chechnya*. She was found dead in Moscow in 2006.

Real freedom of the press also requires that no owner (or state) has a monopoly over, or owns too much of, the press, as there need to be multiple owners to ensure all views and interests are represented in the stories that reach the public. In Australia, for example, media diversity rules limit how much of the media any owner can control in each geographical area according to a points system, something that other countries could consider adopting.

The threat of the super-injunction

AN INJUNCTION IS a court order preventing the media from reporting something that happens in court. The typical reason for this is that to report the information could prejudice the court proceedings. This usually means that the media can report that something has happened but that they are not allowed to give the details. In contrast, super-injunctions prevent the media from reporting even that there are restrictions – that is, they are not allowed to say that there is something they are not allowed to say. And the use of this kind of super-injunction is on the rise. The *Guardian* reported in October 2009 that it had been served with at least twelve notices of injunctions that could not be reported that year, more than ever before.

The Trafigura case in 2009 brought this kind of injunction to the public's notice. An MP, Paul Farrelly (Newcastle-under-Lyme), asked a question in Parliament about an injunction obtained by oil traders Trafigura and their solicitors Carter-Ruck that tried to prevent stories being published about a report into alleged dumping of toxic waste in the Ivory Coast. According to a timeline of the case published in the *Guardian*, the waste was allegedly dumped in 2006 by a cargo ship chartered by Trafigura, and following the dumping thousands of people in the region reported illnesses including breathing problems, sickness, and diarrhoea.

In 2007 a British lawyer began a group action on behalf of these people, and Trafigura, whilst denying any liability, paid £100 million to the Ivorian government in order to remove the waste, which they said had been dumped by an independent contractor they had appointed in good faith.

In 2009 the *Guardian*, having seen internal Trafigura emails showing advance knowledge that the waste could be hazardous, published what it said was evidence that Trafigura had attempted to cover up the scale of the pollution, and that week Trafigura agreed to pay compensation to each of the people believed to have been made ill.

When Farrelly asked a question about this in Parliament, however, the law firm Carter-Ruck, representing Trafigura, tried to prevent the *Guardian* from reporting the question, and tried to use a super-injunction to prevent the reporting of the existence of an injunction. This was not only futile, as Farrelly's question was a matter of public record, but it attempted to overturn the right to report what takes place in Parliament, a right that has been enshrined in law for centuries.

The case highlighted the power of the online world to ensure freedom of the press when *Guardian* editor Alan Rusbridger wrote a post on the website Twitter that hinted at the existence of the super-injunction. It said: 'Now Guardian prevented from reporting parliament for unreportable reasons. Did John Wilkes live in vain?' John Wilkes was an eighteenth-century journalist who risked his life to win the right to report proceedings in Parliament. By the time Rusbridger had dinner with friends and arrived home, he later wrote in an article about the case, Twitter users had tracked down the relevant parliamentary question and published it all over the internet. By the next day 'Trafigura' was one of the most searched for words on the internet in Europe. In part this was due to celebrity Stephen Fry drawing the attention of his over 800,000 followers on Twitter to the case. Shortly before the case was due in court, Trafigura dropped their attempt to prevent publication.

Take Action

▶ *Help protect persecuted journalists.* Reporters Without Borders (Reporters Sans Frontières) run petitions on their website to help persecuted journalists. Sign them.

▶ *Spread the word.* When you hear that an article, video, or other piece of work is being censored, use the power of the internet to spread it. Once a story gets online, it is hard to close down all links to it, so you are beating the censors – especially if you can find a way to keep the material alive after the original page is pulled offline. You can use whatever type of social media you favour – be it Twitter, Facebook, your own blog, other social media sites, or just emailing the link, with a short synopsis of what it says, to your friends and contacts.

▶ *Become a citizen journalist.* Write down or film what you see. Take a digital video camera or audio recorder with you when you go to public meetings. Put your account online or submit it to old-fashioned news organizations. Just remember always to protect yourself by being accurate in what you report and getting as much detail as possible about anyone you quote.

Where to Get Started

Reporters Without Borders defends journalists and media workers imprisoned or persecuted for doing their job, fights against censorship and laws that undermine press freedom, and works to improve the safety of journalists.
47 rue vivienne
75002 Paris
Tel +33 1 44 83 84 84
www.rsf.org

Index on Censorship promotes freedom of expression around the world.
Free Word Centre
60 Farringdon Road
London EC1R 3GA
Tel 020 7324 2522
www.indexoncensorship.org

Project Censored is a US organization that aims to teach society about the role of a free press in a free society – and to tell the 'news that didn't make the news and why'.
Media Freedom Foundation
PO Box 571
Cotati, CA 94931
USA
Tel +1 708 874 2695
www.projectcensored.org

Down to basics:
Petitions

A petition is a document through which a group of people ask leaders – whether in government, businesses, or social organizations – to take an action. Often, a petition is drawn up by a single person or group and then the general public is canvassed to sign it to indicate that they agree with the petition's demand. For that reason, a petition is one of the easiest campaigning tools to put together: all you need is to identify a demand and provide either a piece of paper or a website on which people can add their names.

But a petition is also one of the hardest tools to pull off effectively, because you have to persuade people to sign your petition and to disclose their personal details on it – something many people are reluctant to do, even in a free society where there are no repercussions for doing so (except, possibly, in the workplace, where your involvement may anger management). The idea is that the signatures act as a show of public support for the demand.

Putting together your petition

Your 'demand' or 'ask' should be very clear so people know exactly what they are putting their name to. This should go at the top and usually begins with the words 'We the undersigned …' Underneath there should be plenty of room for people to sign. Typically people are asked to provide their name in capital letters so it can easily be read, their contact details to verify that they are real people (and so your campaign can contact them with more information later), and their signature. The lines of the petition should be clearly numbered so it can be seen at a glance how many signatures there are.

Somewhere on the petition (on each page of paper or on the website), you should also include a notice letting people know that you might contact them in the future about the campaign – to let them know about a victory, to share more information, or to ask for their help again.

Your petition should look something like this:

We the undersigned urge the sun to shine more often so that we have a hot summer.

	Name	Address	Email	Signature
1.	Joe Bloggs	123 Acacia Close, London	joe@bloggs.com	*Joe Bloggs*
2.	Jane Doe	321 Acacia Rd, Glasgow	Jane@doe.com	*Jane Doe*
3.				
4.				
5.				

The Hot Summer Campaign may contact you in the future with updates on our progress.

Delivering your petition

If you are submitting your petition to an elected body such as your local council, Parliament, or the European Parliament, there may be specific guidelines on the wording of the petition that should be followed – these can usually be found on the website of the relevant institution.

There are many websites that let you create petitions online and circulate them by email; these change frequently but a simple web search for 'online petition' will take you to several options. Even if you take your petition online, it is good to have a paper version for people who do not use email.

The number of signatures you need to collect entirely depends on the nature of the petition. If your demand involves something in your village, then an effective petition would likely not need more signatures than the number of residents in the village. Yet some petitions can receive tens of thousands or hundreds of thousands of signatures. For example, a petition circulated in 2008 by Darfuri refugees asking then Prime Minister Gordon Brown to support a UN peacekeeping force to enter and end the violence in the Darfur region of Sudan got over 30,000 signatures, many from people for whom the act of signing the petition could endanger their lives.

When you feel you have collected enough signatures, you need to present the petition to its target. If you've used a paper petition, you'll often need to hand over the original, so make a photocopy for your records.

If you can, set up a meeting with the person you will be giving the petition to, so that you can share more information about your campaign at the same time.

There is a long tradition of petitions being delivered directly to the door of Number 10 Downing Street, the home of the British prime minister. You can't just turn up of course – this needs to be arranged in advance through the Downing Street Petitions Office (Tel 0207 321 7154) who will carry out security checks and arrange a day and time for you to deliver your signatures.

6

Fight racism

Though the slave trade was abolished in the nineteenth century and Apartheid ceased to rule South Africa in 1994, the belief that some people are superior to others because of the colour of their skin or their ethnic background still exists in many forms. In some instances it is found in subtle beliefs that occasionally emerge in conversation, suggesting that someone has a particular personality trait because of his or her race. In other situations it is institutionalized, as in the way an employer may be less likely to interview someone because of a foreign-sounding name or a teacher may assume a student isn't performing well because of his or her background. And in the case of some right-wing political parties, racism is organized – and may turn violent.

Whenever a person or group is discriminated against because of race or ethnicity, it is racism. This includes campaigns against traveller camps or gypsies, assumptions made about asylum seekers, fears that someone is a terrorist because he or she is in an ethnic minority, and stereotypes based on religion. And it also includes nationalized racism such as the French government's policy to dismantle Roma camps and send those without work or residency permits back to Romania and Bulgaria.

We not only have to ensure that these prejudices are not acted on, but that these views are seen as unacceptable as well. This means not buying newspapers that encourage fear, not making assumptions about the skills or interests people will have, and standing up to any racist comments that you hear or read.

Take Action

▶ *Don't collude.* If someone makes a racist comment, even a subtle or unconscious one, speak out and say that you think it is unacceptable.

▶ *Change the institutions.* Check that your school or workplace has an anti-racism policy stating that any discrimination, including racism, is unacceptable and explaining what procedures are in place if discrimination occurs.

▶ *Reach out.* It is hard to view people as different if you know them, so set up sports matches or other events between different communities.

▶ *Report offences.* Campaign against racist political parties, and report any information you hear about their activities in your local community to anti-fascist organizations such as *Searchlight* magazine.

Where to Get Started

The **Equality and Human Rights Commission** protects, enforces, and promotes equality in the areas of age, disability, gender, race, religion and belief, sexual orientation, and gender reassignment. The commission staffs hotlines in England, Scotland, and Wales for dealing with complaints about discrimination and has offices in Cardiff, Glasgow, London, and Manchester.
Helpline (England) 0845 604 6610
Helpline (Scotland) 0845 604 5510
Helpline (Wales) 0845 604 8810
www.equalityhumanrights.com

Kick It Out works to combat racism in football and other sports.
PO Box 29544
London EC2A 4WR
Tel 020 7684 4884
www.kickitout.org

Love Music Hate Racism uses the diverse music scene as a way to involve people in anti-racist and anti-fascist campaigns. You can find a local chapter via their website, or – if you're a musician, know a musician, or want to ask a musician to help out your community – download their

guide to organizing a Love Music Hate Racism gig or event (lovemusichateracism.com/yourevent/).
PO Box 66759
London WC1A 9EQ
Tel 020 7801 2781
www.lovemusichateracism.com

Searchlight **Magazine** is an international anti-fascist magazine.
PO Box 1576
Ilford IG5 0NG
Tel 020 7681 8660
searchlightmagazine.com

7

Reform prisons

The argument for prison reform is based around a fundamental question about the purpose of the penal system: is it simply about punishment and exacting revenge or is it about attempting to make amends for harm done and helping people to change for the better?

Some people say that prison acts as a deterrent, although crime rates year-on-year suggest this is not so. Others say that prison can help people to rehabilitate, and while this seems to be so in some cases, nearly 50 per cent of released prisoners going on to commit further offences. In fact, it is pretty difficult to turn your life around in prison, says Andrew Neilson of the Howard League for Penal Reform, as prisons are violent places, both literally – in terms of prisoners attacking prisoners, staff attacking prisoners, prisoners attacking staff, and prisoners attacking themselves – and in terms of what they do to people's sense of self, of space, and freedom to act.

What's more, as prisons cost money to build and operate, the more people we send to prison the more this means taking money away from social policy solutions that might be far more effective at cutting crime, such as investing in schools, hospitals, public spaces, and access to employment. This can lead to situations like that in California, where the state's prisons budget is bigger than its budget for higher education.

In the acclaimed television show *The Wire*, the character Avon Barksdale is sentenced to seven years in prison on drugs charges, and, having violated the terms of his parole, is told by the cop that he is going to end up having to serve the whole sentence. 'Shit, you only do two days no how. Day you go in ...' says Barksdale, '... and the day you come out' says one of his crew. Prison is, he suggests by this, just a different kind of life and one that you have to get used to, just as you have to reacclimatize to real life on the day you get out.

But prison is only just another type of life if your life on the outside is characterized by a lack of choice and opportunity, and this is what we need to change if prison is to help people change their lives. Otherwise it is just where people who have already been failed by society go to be failed some more.

People are sent to prison to be deprived of their liberty, not their identity or their citizenship. Prisoners must have scope to take responsibility for their own lives, help others and prepare for successful community resettlement
'BARRED CITIZENS', PRISON REFORM TRUST

Take Action

▶ *Help prevent the need for prison*. Become a volunteer for a charity that works with offenders, ex-offenders, and people at risk of offending. Opportunities include providing sports coaching for young people, offering mentoring or peer support to prisoners and vulnerable adults, and supporting young people who have been excluded from school.

▶ *Campaign for the abolition of sentences of twelve months or less* by writing to your MP and to the Ministry of Justice. People on short sentences have usually committed relatively minor offences and may suffer from more complex problems, such as addiction and mental health needs. Around two-thirds of the annual intakes to prison are people with short sentences; they represent about 11 per cent of the prison population at any one time.

▶ *Make some noise about the conditions in prisons.* The world of prisons is particularly secretive, but by using the Freedom of Information Act (see page 48) you can obtain very interesting information on everything from the cost of consultants when a private prison is tendered to the number of self-harm incidents year-on-year in your local prison. You can use this information to get some coverage in the media.

Where to Get Started

The **Howard League for Penal Reform** is the oldest penal reform charity in the UK, established in 1866 and named after John Howard, one of the first prison reform campaigners.
1 Ardleigh Road
London N1 4HS
Tel 020 7249 7373
www.howardleague.org

The **Prison Reform Trust** works to ensure prisons are just, humane, and effective.
15 Northburgh Street
London EC1V 0JR
Tel 020 7251 5070
www.prisonreformtrust.org.uk

Nacro aims to reduce crime by changing lives and they work with offenders and those at risk of offending, to help them find positive alternatives to crime and to achieve their full potential in our society.
Park Place
10–12 Lawn Lane
London SW8 1UD
Tel 020 7840 7200
www.nacro.org.uk

8

Object to discriminatory policing

It would be nice to think that the police are there solely for our protection. For some groups of people, however – and I don't mean criminals – they can be far more of a hindrance than a help.

No case showed this more soberly than the stabbing to death of Stephen Lawrence, a black sixth-former, in South London in 1993. The murder appeared to be racially motivated, and though several suspects were brought in for questioning, none were arrested or charged. In 1999, the independent Macpherson inquiry investigated the police force's actions around this case and found that the service suffered from what he called institutionalized racism. The inquiry recommended seventy reforms, among them the creation of the Race Relations Amendment Act, which requires every public body in the UK to take racism seriously.

Ten years on from the Macpherson inquiry the head of the Equality and Human Rights Commission, Trevor Phillips, announced that he thinks the police are no longer institutionally racist. And it is true that the UK's police service as a whole seems to show greater awareness of diversity than it did, at least publicly. Yet people from the black community are still far more likely than white people to be stopped by the police with no reason for suspicion other than their race and black men tend to be treated differently on arrest: 30 per cent have had their DNA profiles logged on the national DNA database, compared with 10 per cent of white men who have been arrested.

Of course, police discrimination isn't limited to the UK. The

European Union Agency for Fundamental Rights reported that across Europe, someone belonging to a minority group is still more likely to be stopped by police than a person belonging to a country's indigenous population. And the American Civil Liberties Union's Campaign Against Racial Profiling fights against discrimination in the USA, from 'Driving While Black' stops by police to a legal challenge to the 2010 Arizona law that requires police officers to check the immigration status of individuals they stop if they 'suspect they are in the country unlawfully'.

If all communities are to trust the police and view them as a force for good, this kind of discrimination needs to stop and the police need to ensure they are representative of the communities they serve by recruiting more members from ethnic minorities. Only then will they be able to build good relationships with all of the communities they patrol.

Take Action

▶ *Know your rights.* If you or your friends – or people you see on the street – are the subject of discriminatory policing, your best defence is the law. The Citizen Foundation offers a guide to your rights if you are stopped or arrested, including a pocket-sized version. It's easy to carry this primer with you at all times. If you carry two with you, you'll be in a position to share a copy with others if need be.

▶ *Watch the watchers.* Many meetings held by the police authorities to keep a check on each police force, are open to the public. Police authorities offer citizens a chance to register general concerns and get to know the police officers in their community. Attend your local meetings – and speak up.

▶ *File complaints.* If you have a complaint about the behaviour or conduct of police officers and staff and it directly affected you – that is, you were at the scene, rather than seeing it on TV or reading about it on a community website – then you can complain to the Independent Police Complaints Commission (www.ipcc.gov.uk). Be sure to note the 'shoulder number' on the police officers' uniforms and politely ask for their names.

▶ *Use the power of free information.* One of the reasons discriminatory policing persists is because it's easy for most of us to miss it – unless you happen to be one of the people who the police stop and search. But anyone can use the Freedom of Information Act to request information on government agencies, including police forces. Among the most eye-opening statistics: the number of 'stop and search' arrests the police have made in your community during a specific time period, including the gender, race/ethnicity, and other demographic information about the people stopped. See page 48 for more guidance of how to take advantage of the Freedom of Information Act.

Where to Get Started

Citizenship Foundation encourages people to engage directly in their communities and create a more democratic society.
63 Gee Street
London EC1V 3RS
Tel 020 7566 4141
www.citizenshipfoundation.org.uk

The **American Civil Liberties Union** campaigns on a number of human rights issues, including racial profiling, in the USA.
125 Broad Street, 18th Floor
New York, NY 10004
USA
www.aclu.org

Down to basics:
The Freedom of Information Act

The Freedom of Information Act gives everyone the right to ask any public body in England, Wales, and Northern Ireland for any information they might have that you want (Scotland has a similar, independent act). Public authorities include government departments, local authorities and councils, health trusts, hospitals, doctors' surgeries, educational establishments, publicly funded museums, and the police.

To make a request for information you just have to write to or email the relevant public authority, including your name and address and a description of the information you want. Your description should be as detailed as possible so it is better to ask for 'the statistics around spending on paper clips bulldog clips' rather than 'everything you have about stationery'. Providing this information does not fall in one of the categories that the act allows to be withheld, the public authority must comply with your request and should send you the information within twenty working days or write to you if this is not possible and tell you when you will receive it.

Making a Freedom of Information request is normally free, though you can be asked to pay for photocopying or postage. If the public authority thinks it will cost more than a specific amount (£450 or £600 for a request to central government, at the time of writing) then your request can be turned down.

If your request is turned down for any reason you should ask for an internal review of the decision. If the request is still denied, you can appeal against the decision to the independent Information Commissioner.

Keep in mind that information about you held by public authorities is dealt with under the Data Protection Act, not the Freedom of Information Act – the Freedom of Information Act therefore shouldn't be used to find out what information is held about you personally.

More information can be found on the website of the Information Commissioner, www.ico.gov.uk.

9

Kill the death penalty

Fifty-eight countries in the world retain the death penalty as part of their justice system, including the USA. And although capital punishment for murder was suspended in Great Britain in 1969, surveys show that there is significant support for its restoration, especially after high-profile violent crimes. So there's no reason to think that this issue is closed, even in those countries that have banned the practice of capital punishment.

That's pretty surprising since, thanks to the work of organizations such as the New York City-based Innocence Project, the most compelling argument against the death penalty is now well known: because the justice system is not perfect, innocent people may be put to death. And unlike with other miscarriages of justice, an execution cannot be made right. Even if the only people ever executed were guilty of the crimes with which they had been charged, there are compelling arguments against capital punishment. These include the idea that whether you live or die should not depend on the skill of the person defending you, nor should it be the state's job to kill its citizens when its primary job is to protect them. As Amnesty International says in its campaign literature on this subject: 'The death penalty is the ultimate denial of human rights. It is the premeditated and cold-blooded killing of a human being by the state. This cruel, inhuman, and degrading punishment is done in the name of justice. It violates the right to life as proclaimed in the Universal Declaration of Human Rights.' Finally, for those who think it is important as a deterrent, studies consistently show that the threat of the death penalty does not reduce crime. For example, Amnesty cites a *New York Times* study of two decades of crime statistics which show that US states with the death penalty have much higher murder rates than those without it – in some cases more than double. In addition, they report that all fourteen US states without the death penalty have murder rates at or below the US average.

The existence of a death penalty also buys into the idea that the justice system is wholly about punishment. Add into all this the disproportionate number of African American prisoners who are sentenced to death in the USA, as highlighted by the American Civil Liberties Union, and its use becomes pretty indefensible.

International opinion matters on issues like these, and the fact that the death penalty exists anywhere is a poor reflection on all

---

How the justice system fails

Of the death penalty convictions overturned by the Innocence Project using DNA testing evidence – the highest standard of forensic scientific evidence now available:

- 75 per cent of the cases involved 'eyewitnesses' who wrongfully identified the person as the perpetrator. Scientific studies have shown that eyewitnesses are often unreliable, but it's hard for a jury or judge not to be persuaded by such very human evidence.
- 15 per cent involved informants who testified against the defendant, sometimes with hidden incentives such as monetary compensation or a reduction in their own prison sentences.
- 25 per cent of the individuals had made an incriminating statement, false confession, or guilty plea – even though they had not committed the crime.

societies. There should be a concerted international effort to ban capital punishment everywhere, with no exceptions. As Amnesty International put it, this should be regardless of the nature of the crime, the characteristics of the offender, or the method used by the state to kill the prisoner.

Take Action

▶ *Appeal to save a life*. Write to people in authority when the death penalty is handed out in a case, when a death penalty appeal is being considered, and when an execution is imminent. Depending on the time you have available, you can either focus on one or two specific cases – sending appeals to a range of authorities and public figures who may hold sway – or sign up to Amnesty International's Urgent Action network (see page 54) or the National Coalition to Abolish the Death Penalty's action alerts.

▶ *Lobby on the law*. If you live in or come from a country where the death penalty exists, write, call, or meet with elected representatives to share your objections to its use. When a case is in the news, take the opportunity to write a letter to the editor or an opinion piece for your local newspapers, making the case for why the death penalty isn't good for the community.

▶ *Get the word out*. Set up a movie night viewing of *After Innocence*, the award-winning 2005 documentary about seven wrongfully convicted men who were saved from the death penalty through the work of the Innocence Project.

Where to Get Started

Amnesty International declares its mission as 'to protect people wherever justice, fairness, freedom, and truth are denied'. Their work includes campaigning against the death penalty in all its forms.

Human Rights Action Centre
17–25 New Inn Yard
London EC2A 3EA
Tel 020 7033 1500
www.amnesty.org.uk

The **American Civil Liberties Union** campaigns on a number of human rights issues, including the death penalty, in the USA.
125 Broad Street, 18th Floor
New York, NY 10004
USA
Tel +1 212 000 0000
www.aclu.org

The **Innocence Project** was founded by Barry C. Scheck and Peter J. Neufeld in 1992 at Yeshiva University in New York City to assist prisoners who could be proven innocent through DNA testing. To date, 254 people in the USA have been exonerated by DNA testing, including seventeen who served time on death row.
100 Fifth Avenue, 3rd Floor
New York, NY 10011
Tel +1 212 364 5340
USA
www.innocenceproject.org

The **National Coalition to Abolish the Death Penalty** (NCADP) was founded in 1976 in response to the Supreme Court decision in *Gregg v. Georgia* which permitted executions to resume in the USA. Their mission is to abolish the death penalty across the USA and to support efforts to abolish the death penalty worldwide.
1705 DeSales Street NW, 5th Floor
Washington, DC 20036
USA
Tel +1 202 331 4090
www.ncadp.org

Reprieve campaigns for the human rights of prisoners and provides legal assistance to British nationals facing the death penalty around the world.
PO Box 52742
London EC4P 4WS
Tel 020 7353 4640
www.reprieve.org.uk

Down to basics:
The Urgent Action alert

An Urgent Action is one of many campaigning tools employed by Amnesty International. It is used when the organization receives news of someone in danger and thinks that an immediate mass public response could have an impact. This includes cases of people at risk of ill treatment, death threats, the death penalty, 'disappearance', forced repatriation, extrajudicial execution, torture, unacknowledged detention, and denial of access to legal counsel.

Activists are usually asked to send a fax, email, or letter to the authorities in the country where the person is in danger. The authorities concerned thus receive thousands of pieces of communication from across the globe, some arriving minutes after activists have been informed, some up to six weeks later, ensuring the country knows that people across the world are watching them. This means ordinary people can take action in a way that might make a tangible difference in saving the life of someone at risk.

To join Amnesty International's Urgent Action network visit their website, www.amnesty.org.uk. The site also includes tips for writing letters to government officials when speed is of the essence.

10

Campaign against torture

Torture, or the use of cruel, inhumane, and degrading treatment, has been used throughout history to extract information from people. In 1929, the newly formed United Nations crafted the Third Geneva Convention, which insisted on the humane treatment of all prisoners of war, and in 1949 the Fourth Geneva Convention extended these protections to civilians, as well. The Geneva Conventions have been ratified by 194 nations – but unfortunately, that has not led to the end of the use of torture. Torture is routinely used to silence political dissenters in authoritarian states. In recent years, human rights watchdogs have accused the governments of France, Germany, the UK, and the USA of torturing prisoners or being complicit in the use of torture by others – and in all but the USA, there have been official investigations into the use of torture in Afghanistan, Iraq, and elsewhere, as part of the 'war on terror'.

The use of torture is wrong for many reasons. There is the inherent moral wrongness of inflicting pain on another human being. According to Douglas Johnson, the director of the Center for the Victims of Torture and a member of the advisory panel for the prevention of torture of the Organization for Security and Co-operation in Europe, survivors of torture suffer severe physical pain, depression, anxiety disorders, suicidal tendencies, and other symptoms throughout their lives. Then there is the effect torture has on the torturer; using torture dehumanizes those who carry it out as well as those who are tortured.

Thankfully, it's hard to find people who will argue that torture is moral. However, proponents of 'harsh interrogation techniques' – which include such infamous practices as water-boarding, which the United Nations does classify as 'torture' – say that if the information gained can be used for the greater good, then the techniques are a necessary evil. Yet there is the question of whether information gained under physical or emotional coercion is actually true; tortured people may say anything to stop their pain, including confessing to crimes they have not committed, revealing plots that do not exist, and falsely implicating innocent people.

To end torture around the globe, we must start at home. We need to ensure that our own government utterly condemns all forms of torture and does not participate in the transfer of prisoners to countries where torture is used. We must also keep pressure on the government to ensure that evidence gained through torture is not allowed to be used in courts.

This is a day on which we pay our respects to those who have endured the unimaginable. This is an occasion for the world to speak up against the unspeakable. It is long overdue that a day be dedicated to remembering and supporting the many victims and survivors of torture around the world

UNITED NATIONS SECRETARY-GENERAL KOFI ANNAN,
ON THE FIRST UN INTERNATIONAL DAY IN SUPPORT OF VICTIMS OF TORTURE

Take Action

▶ *Make a day of your support.* The UN marks its International Day in Support of Victims of Torture annually on 26 June. Choose this day to raise money for an organization that helps victims of torture or to write to your representatives about the issue.

▶ *Volunteer your services.* If you are a qualified doctor, therapist, psychologist, psychotherapist, or counsellor, then you may be able to volunteer through the Medical Foundation for the Care of Victims of Torture or a similar NGO.

▶ *Address the ambassadors.* Whenever there are reports that a country has been involved with torture, write to the country's ambassadors in your own country to protest against the actions. If you live in France, Germany, the UK, or the USA, send a copy of your letter to your own representative, along with a second letter asking that your government open its files on its involvement in torture and forcefully condemn torture at home and elsewhere.

Where to Get Started

The **Medical Foundation for the Care of Victims of Torture** gives medical and psychological treatment and practical assistance to people who have been tortured and helps to educate the public and decision makers about torture and its consequences.
111 Isledon Road
Islington
London N7 7JW
Tel 020 7697 7777
www.torturecare.org.uk

Amnesty International campaigns against the use of torture as well as other injustices and human rights abuses around the world.
Human Rights Action Centre
17–25 New Inn Yard
London EC2A 3EA
Tel 020 7033 1500
www.amnesty.org.uk

Founded in 1985, the **Center for Victims of Torture** offers rehabilitation services for survivors of torture, including medical and psychological treatment and peer counselling training at refugee camps in Africa and elsewhere in the world. They have assisted 18,000 torture survivors.
2356 University Avenue West, Suite 430
St. Paul, MN 55114
USA
Tel +1 612 436 4800
www.cvt.org

11

Be kind to refugees and migrants

In the West, most of us have had the luck to live in peacetime and have only been ruled by a democratically elected government. So it's easy to forget that this isn't the case for many people. There is nothing more frightening than your own government persecuting you, or being unable to protect you, and having to flee the country you call home. What's more, after hazardous journeys to escape persecution, refugees then often face layers of bureaucracy they do not understand, a language that is completely new, economic hardship, and possible detention. Add to this hostility in the press, from politicians, and from people living in the towns where they are sent and you can start to imagine the terrifying and demoralizing ordeal they must face.

For economic migrants who leave their homes not because of persecution but in search of work or a better standard of living for themselves and their families, the experience can be just as frightening. EU expansion saw 1.4 million East Europeans moving to the UK between 2004 and 2008. In many cases such migration is encouraged to help fill gaps in the workforce, yet many economic migrants face xenophobia and racism. This is not only morally wrong, but misses the fact that migration can have a positive impact on our society, adding billions of pounds in taxes to the budget and still more in contributions sent back to migrants' home communities.

If we left our homes and our communities and went in search of a better life, wouldn't we want some kindness to be shown to us?

Take Action

▶ *Reach out.* Contact a local refugee centre and set up a game of football or other sport between anyone at the centre who is interested and you and your mates. Playing sport is one of the best ways people share a common experience, feel part of a community, and make friends.

▶ *Know the terminology.* Under international law there is no such thing as an 'illegal asylum seeker'. Challenge people who use incorrect terms as a way of keeping refugees separate from the larger community. If you read or hear a media report that uses misleading terminology, write a 'letter to the editor' and explain why they are wrong.

▶ *Learn the facts.* Did you know that the UK is home to just 2 per cent of the world's 16 million refugees? And that African and Asian countries host more than three-quarters of the global refugee population? The Refugee Council website (www. refugeecouncil.org.uk) offers lots of information about the real lives of refugees in our country – which doesn't always match the rhetoric in public debate.

Where to Get Started

The **Refugee Council** gives direct help and support to refugees and asylum seekers and works with them to ensure their needs and concerns are addressed.
240–250 Ferndale Road
Brixton
London SW9 8BB
Tel 020 7346 6700
www.refugeecouncil.org.uk

The **Joint Council for the Welfare of Immigrants** (JCWI) campaigns for justice in immigration, nationality, and refugee law and policy. Their overarching objective is to relieve poverty and hardship among immigrants and refugees by promoting their human, economic, and civil rights.
115 Old Street
London EC1V 9RT
Tel 020 7251 8708
www.jcwi.org.uk

Get to know refugees, immigrants, and migrants

ASYLUM SEEKER: A person who has left his or her country of origin and formally applied for asylum in another country but whose application has not yet been finally decided. Asylum seekers can appeal against a rejected application in the courts, and in 2009 the UK courts overturned 28 per cent of the applications that were originally denied.

REFUGEE: A person who has proved that he or she would face persecution at home and whose asylum application to remain in another country has been accepted.

'FAILED' ASYLUM SEEKER: A person whose asylum application has failed and who has no other protection claim awaiting a decision. Some refused asylum seekers voluntarily return to their home country, while others are forcibly returned. For some it is not safe or practical to return to their home country until conditions there change.

'ILLEGAL' IMMIGRANT: Someone whose entry into or presence in a country contravenes immigration laws.

ECONOMIC MIGRANT: Someone who has moved to another country to work.

Source: Refugee Council. Reprinted with permission.

Principled activism:
The classic rules of organizing

David Russell is Director of Survivors' Fund (www.survivors-fund.org.uk), which supports and campaigns for survivors of the Rwandan genocide. Inspired by Saul Alinsky's classic guidebook to organizing, *Rules for Radicals: A Pragmatic Primer for Realistic Radicals* (1971), he has developed the following principles for effective campaigns:

- Power is perception. Power is what your opponents think you have, over and above the power you actually do have.
- Don't be afraid to ridicule your opponents, if their position is untenable.
- Campaigning should be enjoyable. It keeps your followers engaged.
- Persistence does pay. Keep focused on your goal, but vary your tactics to keep the campaign fresh.
- Decide who to campaign against, and make it personal. If the individuals won't take responsibility, then work to ensure they do.

12

Make businesses act responsibly

Corporate Social Responsibility (CSR) has become something of a hip business buzzword, so much so that most businesses are falling over themselves to talk about their CSR credentials. CSR means that the company is not just about making money but is also interested in doing good for society generally. It is the umbrella phrase for what businesses might call 'putting something back' or 'being part of the community'. How a business does this varies from company to company but it can include contracting with environmentally sound suppliers, using Fairtrade produce where possible, or ensuring no child labour is used. Or it could mean having a diversity and equal opportunities policy in place, giving staff paid days off to help charitable causes, or donating a share of the profits to charity.

But while many companies like to boast about their CSR credentials, it can take a lot of public pressure to make them actually put their money where their mouth is. Take BP, the petroleum giant that spent millions of dollars advertising its environmentally friendly projects. On 20 April 2010, a blowout occurred on the company's Deepwater Horizon offshore rig, spilling 50,000 gallons of BP's crude oil into the Gulf of Mexico each day, for nearly three months. That added up to nearly 4.9 million barrels of oil, the largest oil spill in history. Public and government anger at the way BP handled the accident led the company to establish a $20-billion compensation fund to assist individuals and businesses directly affected by the mess.

As a consumer, you can encourage your favourite companies to adopt more CSR practices that actually matter; as a shareholder, you can check to see that the companies you invest in do so, too.

Take Action

▶ *Make your company responsible.* Encourage your company to think about the environmental impact of its work. Introduce environmentally friendly policies such as recycling paper and ink cartridges, turning off lights and computers when the office is empty or when they are not being used, and buying materials from environmentally friendly suppliers. Ask your employer to offer incentives or financial bonuses to those staff who use public transport to travel to work.

▶ *Solicit corporate involvement.* If you are working on a campaign or volunteering for a charity, ask the businesses in the area to support your work. Help them by coming up with a list of ways a company can get involved, from providing donations of surplus inventory to letting their staff help you during paid work hours.

▶ *Ask for better reporting.* In 2008, Denmark's parliament passed a law requiring that the largest corporations in the country – whether publicly or privately owned – list standardized CSR information in their annual reports, including the results of their CSR efforts. Track down whether a CSR project is more than just window-dressing, and let other people know, too. Then petition the company to make the project's public relations into a reality.

Where to Get Started

The **Fairtrade Foundation** works to improve the livelihoods of farmers and other producers in the southern hemisphere by certifying and raising public awareness around Fairtrade products. They provide resources for universities and schools, workplaces, and community groups to increase the use of Fairtrade products.
3rd Floor, Ibex House
42–47 Minories
London EC3N 1DY
Tel 020 7405 5942
www.fairtrade.org.uk

Corporate Watch undertakes research on the social and environmental impact of large corporations, particularly multinationals, and publishes a newsletter to keep people informed of their research.
Freedom Press
Angel Alley
84b Whitechapel High Street
London E1 7QX
Tel 020 7426 0005
www.corporatewatch.org.uk

Get to know refugees, immigrants, and migrants

What is Fairtrade?

FAIRTRADE IS ABOUT better prices, decent working conditions, local sustainability, and fair terms of trade for farmers and workers in the developing world. By requiring companies to pay sustainable prices (which must never fall lower than the market price), Fairtrade addresses the injustices of conventional trade, which traditionally discriminates against the poorest, weakest producers. It enables them to improve their position and have more control over their lives.

What is the Fairtrade Mark?

The Fairtrade Mark is an independent consumer label which appears on UK products as a guarantee that they have been certified against internationally agreed

Fairtrade standards. It shares internationally recognized Fairtrade standards with initiatives in twenty other countries, working together globally with producer networks such as Fairtrade Labelling Organisations International (FLO). The Mark indicates that the product has been certified to give a better deal to the producers involved – it does not act as an endorsement of an entire company's business practices

How many Fairtrade products are there in the UK?

The Fairtrade Foundation has licensed over 3000 Fairtrade certified products for sale through retail and catering outlets in the UK.

Can buying Fairtrade products help to tackle climate change?

The Fairtrade system includes environmental standards as part of producer certification. The standard requires producers to work to protect the natural environment and make environmental protection a part of farm management. Producers are also encouraged to minimize the use of energy, especially energy from non-renewable sources.

In addition, by purchasing Fairtrade products, shoppers in the UK are ensuring that producer organizations receive a Fairtrade premium for investment in economic, social, and environmental products of their own choice. These premiums can enable farmers to implement a range of environmental protection programmes which will contribute to the range of solutions needed to address climate change and ultimately benefit all of us. To give two examples, tea workers in India have invested some of their Fairtrade premium into replacing the traditional wood-burning heating with a solar-panelled system. Coffee farmers in Costa

Rica have used the premium to replant trees to prevent soil erosion and have invested in environmentally friendly ovens, fuelled by recycled coffee hulls and the dried shells of macadamia nuts. This means that they no longer need to cut forest trees and so can preserve the rainforest and the oxygen they produce.

By choosing Fairtrade products, you can therefore help producers preserve their own environment as well as have a positive social benefit in their community.

Reproduced with permission from the Fairtrade Foundation.

Protecting people:
How the message matters

Elaine Londesborough-van Rooyen is Campaigning Manager at Cancer Research UK (www.cancerresearchuk.org). She worked on the campaign for smokefree workplaces which resulted in England's 'smoking ban'. This was introduced in 2007 and made it illegal to smoke in enclosed public places.

Q *Can you explain what kind of smoking ban you wanted?*

A We wanted smokefree public places but initially there was concern from the public and from policy makers because it was seen as too 'nanny-state'. When we made the campaign about protecting people who worked in a smoky environment, it got more support. The main message of the Smokefree Workplaces campaign was 'working is not a crime; it shouldn't carry a death sentence'.

Q *Was this something Cancer Research UK did by itself?*

A No, we worked as part of a coalition called Smokefree Action Coalition – a wide-ranging group of organizations such as the British Heart Foundation, British Lung Foundation, British Medical Association, and the anti-smoking charity ASH (Action on Smoking and Health). It was important that we showed a united front on something that was so high profile and against the strong opposition of the tobacco industry and groups like Forest, a smokers' campaign group.

Q *How did you involve the public?*

A We collected signatures on petitions and asked people to write to their MP. We also gave people templates to write to the Department of Health in response to their consultation on smoke-free legislation. Writing to a government department on this kind of issue was quite a new thing to do, and around half of the total responses to the consultation came from Cancer Research UK supporters. In total about 25,000 people got involved in the campaign in one way or another.

Q *Did you use any stunts?*

A We did lots of press work, photocalls, and stunts. Alongside the more traditional briefings in the last few days before Parliament decided on whether to introduce the ban, we sent fake cigarette packets to every MP that had hard-hitting health warnings printed on them. Because the government was backing a plan to allow smoking to continue in pubs that didn't serve food, we also organized a media photocall outside Parliament involving a tug of war between a giant pizza slice and a giant cigarette that highlighted how pubs would have to choose between food and smoking.

Q *Were MPs influenced by public opinion?*

A The vote on whether to introduce a smoking ban was in February 2006. Over 90 per cent of MPs received around fifteen letters or emails from constituents asking them to support the smoking ban in the last few days before the vote. Anecdotally many MPs have told us that these letters helped them to make up their minds as the vote in the House of Commons was a free vote – which means MPs did not have to adhere to the party line. The legislation passed with a majority of over 200. And in 2007 all enclosed public places became smokefree.

13

Insist on better banking

The credit crunch may have focused everyone's minds on banks, but better banking is an idea to shout about whatever the economic climate. It's about making sure that all people can access fair finance, not just the well off, and about ensuring the banking system gives back to society by investing in the areas that need it most. According to the Better Banking Campaign coalition of over 500 organizations, nearly 6 million people in the UK are unable to access mainstream credit. This isn't necessarily because they have a bad banking history but because they have no credit history. If they need to borrow money they have to seek out other lenders, some of which charge interest rates of up to 9000 per cent. Better banking gives all of us, not just the well off, access to mortgages, loans, and other credit on fair terms, and ensures that banks invest in the neighbourhoods where finance is most needed.

The campaign for better banking has three demands:

- transparency from banks about the communities they do and don't serve;
- an incentive structure to encourage banks to fully engage with people and businesses in all communities; and
- a cap on extortionate lending rates and a commitment from banks to re-invest 1 per cent of their profits for social benefit.

This campaign isn't about putting bricks through banks' windows, as some protestors have been known to do on anti-capitalist riots. It's about trying to make the system in which we live fairer and accessible to everyone. It's about stopping unfair bank charges. It's about protecting people from unscrupulous lenders. And it's about ensuring the balance of power lies with consumers and not with the banks. Given the recent history of banks needing government bailouts while bankers continue to receive huge bonuses, this seems the least they can do.

> *A bank is a place where they lend you an umbrella in*
> *fair weather and ask for it back when it begins to rain*
> ROBERT FROST

Take Action

▶ *Move your money.* Check out which banks have ethical policies (these should be trumpeted on their websites) and set up your account with them. After you've switched your account, write to your original bank and tell them why you have moved your money. Nothing makes a bank more likely to change its credit and loan policies than a large number of customers defecting to a competitor.

▶ *Join a credit union.* Credit unions are member-owned financial co-operatives. They offer ethical loans and other banking services to specific groups of people. A credit union may be for people who live locally, work for the same employer, or belong to the same trade union. If there isn't a credit union in your area, you might even consider starting one – though this is a huge task, so not to be done lightly.

▶ *Take from the rich, give to the poor.* Sign up to support the campaign for a Robin Hood Tax, a levy on financial transactions with the money raised to be used to aid development and tackle climate change.

Where to Get Started

Created in 2009, the **Better Banking Campaign** is a coalition of nearly 500 organizations that campaigns to address 'the problem of financial exclusion: the lack of fair access to financial services and credit to those who warrant it'. Coalition leaders include ACEVO (the Association of Chief Executives of Voluntary Organisations), the Centre for Responsible Credit, the Community Development Finance Association, the Development Trust Association, Fair Finance, the London Rebuilding Society, Urban Form, and the investment management provider CCLA.
www.betterbanking.org.uk

The **Association of British Credit Unions** is the trade group for credit unions based in England, Scotland, and Wales. It provides information on existing credit unions and also advises people on how to set one up.
Holyoake House
Hanover Street
Manchester M60 OAS
Tel 016 1832 3694
www.abcul.coop

The **Robin Hood Tax Campaign** is a coalition of organizations and individuals working to reduce poverty around the world and to broker a 'new deal between banks and society' in the wake of the financial crisis. Among the organizations signed on to the coalition are Action Aid, Oxfam, and Stamp Out Poverty.
www.robinhoodtax.org.uk

The **Center for Responsible Lending** is a US organization working to eliminate abusive financial practices. It works with Self-Help, one of America's largest non-profit community development lenders, to create ownership and economic opportunity in underserved communities through responsible loans and financial services.
302 West Main Street
Durham, NC 27701
USA
Tel +1 919 313 8500
www.responsiblelending.org

The bottom line:
Taking on multinational companies where it hurts

Wes Streeting was vice president of the National Union of Students (NUS) in 2007, when the bank HSBC announced a change in its banking policies for recently graduated students. He started a campaign to get the bank to reverse this decision by threatening the very thing it was trying to improve: its profits.

Q *What did HSBC do and why was it a problem?*

A From the moment they start university, all undergraduates typically get an interest-free overdraft as part of banks' efforts to recruit them, with the idea being that people who open accounts as students often stay with that bank for the rest of their lives. But in the summer of 2007 HSBC announced very suddenly that they would be withdrawing the interest-free facility for people who had graduated that year, whereas what normally happens is banks reduce the interest-free entitlement over a few years to give graduates the chance to start paying it off once they start earning money.

This worried us because it was such a sudden and immediate reversal of policy and would set a precedent that other banks might follow. Graduates were starting to get letters saying their interest-free overdraft would be withdrawn in a matter of months. We were worried about graduate hardship, because not everyone gets a job straight after university.

Q *What did the NUS decide to do?*

A The first thing we did was set up a Facebook group called 'Stop the great HSBC graduate rip-off!'. The strength of the NUS is how many members we have, but because the change happened over the summer we knew people wouldn't be on campus and some might be abroad. Plus we needed to find a way of reaching graduates who weren't current students and had left the NUS. Facebook seemed the ideal way to do this. We started to invite as many people as we could to join and asked them to invite other people, too; we soon had over 10,000 group members.

Q *Why was the Facebook group so effective?*

A The Facebook group worked because as the membership increased we started putting advice on the group's wall about how to write a complaint to HSBC; group members themselves did the same, posting about their own experiences and how to close bank accounts. The wall became a place for users to interact with each other, take personal ownership of the campaign, and invite their friends. In fact, HSBC told as that as the group grew, they saw an increase in the number of people going into branches to close accounts and switch to other banks.

This was combined with the NUS putting its resources behind the campaign. We used our media contacts to promote the Facebook group, organized protests, and threatened to ban the bank from freshers' fairs.

Q *What was HSBC's response?*

A We had a convention planned to talk about NUS campaigns for the coming year and we decided that this should coincide with a protest at the HSBC offices. But before this happened, HSBC contacted us to say they would reverse their policy and that anyone who had been charged would have their charges reversed. So we called off the protest.

We then went in to meet HSBC and they expressed an enormous amount of regret and humility. They were really shocked at the strength of feeling over their policy change and hadn't anticipated the reaction it got. They were worried about all the negative publicity they were getting because it came at a time that they were targeting school leavers to open an account before going to university. Not only did they honour their promise but they also sponsored some research on the student experience which they funded to the tune of £330,000 over three years.

14

Demand a living wage for all

What stuff do you need, really need, to buy in order to have an adequate quality of life? You need to be able to pay for somewhere to live and for the heat, water, and electricity for this place. You also need clothing and, assuming you want to keep your job and your friends, the ability to wash these clothes. That also goes for personal hygiene items, such as toothpaste and tampons, shampoo and razors. Then there's the cost of transporting yourself to work and, if you're lucky, some money set aside for emergencies, in case that roof of yours falls in. You might like to add a little extra for some recreation – the bus fare to the park, or perhaps the occasional cinema ticket. And all of this is what you need before you begin to think about any dependants and their needs. A 'living wage' is the term used to describe how much someone needs to earn per hour to afford this level of comfort, if he or she works a forty-hour week and has no additional income.

Remember, this isn't to lead a life of luxury. It doesn't even necessarily pay enough to allow for a TV license, a shop-bought sandwich, or treats or presents. In London the living wage in 2010 was calculated at £7.60 an hour; in New York City it is $10.00 an hour for a job with health insurance benefits or $11.50 an hour for a job without them. These figures are more than the legal minimum wage in both cities, which means that for many people affording the most basic of their needs is barely manageable.

Take Action

▶ *Check where your tips go.* When you're eating out, ask serving staff whether they get the tip if you pay by credit or debit card, and if they don't then leave your tip in cash. Even better, ask the manager of your favourite restaurant to ensure that their policy on service charges and gratuities is clearly noted on their menus.

▶ *Pay a living wage.* If you employ a cleaning company or other business to do work around your house, check that everyone working for it is receiving a living wage – and don't rely on the word of the head office or a project manager. If it doesn't pay a living wage, shift your business elsewhere, and let the company know why you've done so.

▶ *Make a living wage.* Don't accept work for less than the living wage even if it's a short-term holiday or part-time job. If all the people they want to hire demand a living wage, employers will be forced to pay one, even if it isn't the law.

Where to Get Started

London Citizens spearheads the living wage campaign in the UK.
112 Cavell Street
London E1 2JA
Tel 020 7043 9881
www.londoncitizens.org.uk

Living Wage NYC campaigns for a living wage in New York City, which has the highest cost of living in the USA.
30 East 29th Street
New York, NY 10016
USA
Tel +1 212–684–5300
www.livingwagenyc.org

15

Close the wealth gap

There is plenty of evidence to show that in countries where the gap between the rich and the poor is large, everybody suffers the consequences. There are more murders, higher rates of mental illness, and lower rates of literacy than in countries where the wealth gap is narrower. Even those who are the richest in these societies have more problems – including a lower life expectancy – than the richest people in countries where the wealth gap is not so big.

For almost two decades, Britain has been one of the most unequal of the world's richest countries. The minimum wage for a worker in the UK is £5.80 per hour at the time of writing. Compare this to some employees in the banking sector who receive more than a million pounds a year in pay and bonuses. Even if you calculate based on an eighty-hour week, a million pounds a year, worked over forty-eight weeks a year, earns over £260 per hour – more than forty times the earnings of a worker at minimum wage, many of whom have no choice but to take on two jobs to make ends meet.

The bigger the wealth gap is, the bigger it will get. In the housing market, for example, we get super-landlords who can outbid everyone else when it comes to buying housing stock. If the very rich can afford property and most people can't, it adds to the wealth gap.

Ultimately, the argument for closing the wealth gap is about fairness. Why should one person have so much more than another? In the school playground if a child has fifty lollies merely because her parents have spoiled her, wouldn't we ask her to give a lolly or two to a child who has none, to avoid fights, frustrations, anxieties, and bullying? Why shouldn't we take the same approach with grown-ups, too?

Take Action

▶ *Negotiate*. If you work for a private company and are a member of the recognized trade union (which means the company has agreed to negotiate with it), ask your union to demand more seats for employee representatives on the remuneration committee. If you're not a member, then turn to the next campaign!

▶ *Disclose*. Share your wage information anonymously on one of the websites that collates this information, such as My Salary (www.mysalary.co.uk). This will allow people to examine how their earnings compare with others working for the same company and in the same industry, particularly in publicly traded businesses which must publish the salaries of their executives. Don't be afraid to tell others what you earn too, making it easier for everyone to negotiate better wages and harder for companies to pay people differently for doing the same job.

▶ *Discuss*. Invite your friends to a reading group discussion of *The Spirit Level: Why Equality Is Better for Everyone* by Professors Richard Wilkinson and Kate Pickett. At the Equality Trust website, you'll find papers responding to critiques of the book, as well as PowerPoint slides walking through the statistics, that can spur your conversation.

> *If a free society cannot help the many who are poor,*
> *it cannot save the few who are rich*
> JOHN F KENNEDY

Where to Get Started

The Equality Trust runs a programme of public and political
education to encourage widespread
understanding of the harm caused
by income inequality, public
support for policy measures to
reduce income inequality, and
political commitment to implementing such policy measures.
32–36 Loman Street
London SE1 0EH
Tel 020 7922 7927
www.equalitytrust.org.uk

16

Join the trade union movement

In their simplest form, trade unions (or labor unions, as they are known in the USA) are organizations of workers who have joined together to exert greater bargaining power when it comes to their working conditions. But trade unions also serve as an information-sharing channel, campaigning outlet, and training and education provider for employees.

As an employee, many of the rights you currently enjoy probably resulted from the work of unions and their members; successful campaigns include annual leave entitlements, pension contributions, training budgets, parental leave, and protection from bullying. In addition, if you are unfairly sacked from work, your union can advise you and represent you in a tribunal or arbitration to ensure legal processes are followed and to help you get financial compensation.

But since the 1980s, the influence of trade unions has declined, as the sectors of work with the highest union representation – such as manufacturing – have seen job losses, particularly from the relocation of factories overseas, and governments have brought in laws to restrict trade union activities. To hold on to the rights we have, and to lobby for new rights that fit our changing workplaces, we need a thriving trade union movement. Alone, a worker is pretty powerless to protect his or her rights, but as part of a movement with other members of the workforce there is more chance to have a voice and influence.

Take Action

▶ *Find the right union for you.* The Trades Union Congress (TUC) can help you find the most appropriate union for you to join – and there will be one, whatever sector you work in and even if your employer doesn't encourage membership.

▶ *Persuade your workmates to join a union, too.* If your workplace does not recognize a union, it simply takes getting a certain percentage of employees to join the same union in order for you to ask for 'recognition' – that is, when an employer agrees to allow the union to negotiate on behalf of the workforce. The union will be able to advise you on the process.

▶ *Become a rep.* If you are already a member of a trade union consider becoming a union rep, the person whose role it is to promote the union in the workplace and advise and represent people needing the union's help.

Where to Get Started

The **Trades Union Congress** (TUC) is the umbrella organization of Britain's trade unions. Its website gives general information about unions and will point you to the most appropriate union for you to join.
Congress House
Great Russell Street
London WC1B 3LS
Tel 020 7636 4030
www.tuc.org.uk

The **American Federation of Labor and Congress of Industrial Organizations** (AFL-CIO) is an association of fifty-six national and international labor unions. Its website offers a wealth of information on the history of the union movement.
815 16th Street, NW
Washington, DC 20006
USA
www.aflcio.org

The **International Trade Union Confederation** can help you find a union representing your sector in any country around the world. It represents 176 million workers in 156 nations.
Boulevard du Roi Albert II, 5, Bte 1
1210 Brussels
Belgium
Tel +32 (0)2 201 5815
www.ituc-csi.org

Giving workers a voice:
The job of a union rep

Emily Kelly is a civil servant and a workplace representative for the Public and Commercial Services Union (PCS), which represents civil and public servants in central government. The fifth largest union in the UK, PCS has more than 300,000 members in over 200 departments and agencies, as well as staff in parts of government transferred to the private sector.

Q *Why did you become a union rep?*

A My parents taught me to have a healthy disrespect for authority and never to assume that just because someone has more money and status than you they necessarily have good judgement. In my youth I witnessed power cuts, food shortages, and the miners' strike and learnt early on the importance of protest against unfair treatment at work. So when I joined the civil service in 1987, I joined the union straight away. I wanted to be part of the opposition to Margaret Thatcher's rabid conservative government of the time. I've always found union work diverse and challenging and never regretted getting actively involved.

Q *What does being a rep actually involve?*

A My work is never the same on any two days. I'm a full-time rep so that is all I do now, but in many workplaces it is something you do alongside your normal work, with a certain percentage of your hours given over to letting you do this. So you can get involved with your union with whatever commitment you want.

I represent my union at all levels, which involves travelling around the country, speaking to members' meetings, conferences, the media, and in Parliament in order to present our campaigns to the widest possible audience. We campaign on many issues such as job cuts, pensions, pay, and rights for decent working conditions. I also negotiate with management over members' disciplinary and discrimination cases and detrimental changes to members' working conditions. And I write reports and articles for union publications and liaise with other unions and community groups over issues that affect us all, like the public sector cuts programme.

Q *Can you give some examples of how you can help people?*

A When I returned to work after a four-year career break to care for my young children, I helped set up a committee that put together a business case for an onsite nursery and play scheme at my local office. I still feel a sense of accomplishment and pride when a parent at work talks about how important the facility is to them. I would like to think that I have encouraged members to get more involved in their union and stand up for their rights at work. When you feel that you've actually made a positive difference to someone's life it is very rewarding.

Q *Why do you think it's important to join a union?*

A Joining a union gives you a protection at work and collective bargaining procures better working conditions. Without a union you are exposed to someone else's business agenda, which will always be about reducing costs to the detriment of the employee. The union negotiates on pay, pensions, and job security and will if necessary ballot members on strike action if the proposals are unacceptable. The oldest form of protest is to 'down tools', and I have found this is still the most effective way of getting a better deal.

There is a perception that trade unions are dinosaurs and full of middle-aged white males. Well, I've been involved in union work for twenty-three years and as a female single parent, working part-time, I believe that we are active, modern, relevant, and still very much alive.

◆

Richard Messingham currently works as Public Affairs Adviser to a professional membership body, where he is also a UNITE Union workplace representative.

Q *Why did you become a union rep?*

A I have always been interested in the role of unions in the workplace and I have been a member of a trade union since 2005. First I was a member of the public sector union UNISON, and since 2007 I've been a member of UNITE, the largest private-sector union. At a previous employer I had a need for union representation during an employment matter, and I really valued the support, both technical and emotional, that a UNITE rep gave me in a difficult situation. Also, my wider activity in the Labour Party meant for me that joining my workplace trade union was the natural thing to do, and my late grandfather was heavily involved in his union, and also a Labour councillor. Therefore in early 2009 I responded to an email to all UNITE members calling for new reps in my workplace, and was elected unopposed.

Q *What does being a rep actually involve?*

A I am one of the part-time representatives, sometimes called a 'shop steward'. I am also currently chair of the UNITE reps group. Being a part-time rep means that I fulfil this role in addition to my day job. Under the terms of the formal recognition agreement between UNITE and employers, union reps are entitled to spend 10 per cent of their working week on trade union duties, which is called 'facility time'. In exceptional circumstances and with the agreement of Human Resources, this can rise up to 20 per cent. However, my experience has shown that the 3.5 hours allocated is far from enough time. Like most jobs, my work often takes longer than thirty-five hours a week, and I usually have to work on trade union duties over and above my normal workload. However, in some, usually larger or traditionally unionized, work places such as factories and bus garages, the facility time for reps can mean that some reps spend close to 100 per cent of their working week on trade union duties. (I am one of eight potential reps at my workplace, and we are supported by a full-time paid official who works directly for UNITE. He regularly visits our workplace and provides advice and support on our work as reps.)

In addition to the usual facility time, I am also allowed paid leave to attend training courses, and in some circumstances conferences and committee meetings, that directly relate to my role as a rep. However, in some workplaces with a weaker or no recognition agreement, union reps are sometimes only entitled to unpaid leave for these things.

As a rep I also play a role in growing and sustaining the membership of the union in my workplace, through organizing social events, maintaining regular email contact with members, and organizing workplace meetings for members to express their views on issues. In addition, I am also active in the wider work of UNITE, having been elected onto the Regional Committee for the Not for Profit Sector in London, as well as helping out UNITE in its political campaigns during parliamentary and other elections.

Q *Can you give some examples of how you can help people?*

A The bread and butter of my work as a rep is to provide practical advice and emotional support to my members on a variety of workplace issues. This can range from advice on how to make a successful application for flexible working, to dealing with a difficult manager, to supporting members during a redundancy consultation, to, in rarer circumstances, representing a member during a disciplinary hearing. Whilst my role is not to provide expert legal advice, which is for UNITE's lawyers, I can in certain circumstances represent a member during an employment tribunal. Fundamentally, my role is to ensure that the member gets a fair hearing, and that the employer follows its own polices and procedures properly when considering an employment matter.

This work can be challenging and time consuming, particularly when a member's grievance against his or her manager or the disciplinary process against the employee is dragged out over a long period of time. But I start from the firm belief that similar to the role of a lawyer, my member is entitled to a fair hearing and fair representation, and where practical, that member deserves the full support of the union and its resources.

In addition to individual member-related casework, I take a lead on negotiations with management on pay, terms, and conditions. These negotiations, usually with the Chief Executive and Director of Human Resources, are through the Joint Negotiation and Consultative Committee (JNCC), the formal means under the recognition agreement between UNITE and the employer, through which issues are discussed on a confidential basis. JNCC meetings are held every quarter or so. In the autumn, when the annual pay settlement is discussed, they can be more frequent, as reps directly represent our members' views on a realistic pay level for the following twelve months.

Q *Why do you think it's important to join a union?*

A Many workplaces, including mine, suffer from a lack of members putting themselves forward to be a union rep. The reasons are many, including a high workload, family and personal circumstances, and a fear that they will be treated less favourably by management, which in some extreme circumstances may lead to them losing their job. However, it is precisely for these reasons that I think people should join, and be involved in, their workplace union. Only through a significant majority of employees being a member of the union organized in their workplace, will the terms and conditions of employment be improved. A higher density of membership means greater financial resource for the union to help organize effectively in the workplace, and at the same time this means the management of an organization will have to listen the concerns of employees and their union representatives.

17

Care for carers

Caring for others is one of the most natural instincts. Families have always cared for their loved ones, and always will. They want to ensure they get the best possible care, and aren't forced to be in hospital or residential care if they don't want to be there. But being a carer has a big impact on the person's own health, finances, and quality of life, too.

Most carers still keep a job when they become a carer, be it for a child, parent, or partner. But the additional caring duties can stretch the limits of the day, making their lives chaotic, and meaning they are constantly putting other people's needs before their own. Because of this many carers have to give up paid employment.

As a society, we need to support our carers, emotionally and financially. One in eight adults in the UK has a current caring responsibility and those efforts save the economy £87 billion per year, an average of £15,260 per carer. Yet the main carer's benefit is a paltry £53.10 for a minimum of thirty-five hours, equivalent to £1.52 per hour – far short of the national minimum wage.

This also applies to people whose actual jobs are in caring roles. These jobs are amongst the lowest paid, yet involve long hours, shift work, and hard lifting and manual activities. If we ever needed care, we'd want to be treated with dignity and respect – yet we can't expect this unless we treat carers the same way.

We need better financial help for carers, better respite help so that carers get a break, and wider appreciation in society for the important job that carers do.

Take Action

▶ *Investigate the law.* Often when local authorities have to implement national policies regarding financial and other support given to carers in their community, they are given guidance but can exercise a lot of discretion. Find out how your local council is implementing any changes in the law. You can also become a carers' representative on a local group dedicated to patients' rights.

▶ *Help carers in your workplace.* Read your personnel policies and then ask your employers what assistance they give to the carers in your organization. Having flexible work hours can make a big difference to a carer who is juggling family and work. You can be an advocate for a more carer-friendly workplace.

▶ *Learn about the government support available to carers.* Whether you're a carer yourself or know one, you can find out more about entitlements through Carers UK or the Citizens Advice Bureau.

Where to Get Started

Carers UK seeks recognition of the true value of carers' contributions to society. It also campaigns for carers to get the practical, financial, and emotional support they need.
20 Great Dover Street
London SE1 4LX
Tel 020 7378 4999
www.carersuk.org

The **Citizens Advice Bureau** helps people resolve their legal, financial, and other problems by providing free information and advice and influencing policy makers. It can advise you about any benefits and help you might be able to receive as a carer or for a carer in your family. The national administrative office (listed below) does not offer advice, but the location of regional and local field offices and advice hotlines can be found on the organization's website.
Myddelton House
115–123 Pentonville Road
London N1 9LZ
Tel 020 7833 2181
www.citizensadvice.org.uk

18

Help people to achieve a good death

*It's not that I am afraid to die. I just don't want to be
there when it happens*
WOODY ALLEN

What is a 'good death'? Is it the chance to die surrounded by your
loved ones, as free from pain as possible? Or is it dying at a time of
your own choosing, or dying knowing that you've had a chance to
sort out your financial affairs? Maybe you've never considered the
question, or only struggled with it while mourning the loss of a
loved one. There's nothing more personal than how we die and
how we face death. But because nearly all of us are afraid to die –
or because, like Woody Allen, we don't want to be there when it
happens – we tend to put off thinking about how we might make
our deaths as good as possible.

People who choose to take their own life, perhaps due to termi-
nal illness, are often forced to die a lonely death in the absence of
their loved ones due to fear of the legal consequences for anyone
who is present at the time of death. (In England, a conviction for
assisting in a suicide carries a jail sentence of up to fourteen years.)
In recent years, however, highly publicized assisted dying campaigns have helped to change attitudes towards this. And a 2009
BBC film *A Short Stay in Switzerland* told the story of Anne Turner,
a physician suffering from a rare and incurable neurological condition who chose to end her life at the Dignitas Clinic in Switzerland,
which provides legal assisted suicide under the laws there.

For people who prefer to let nature take its course, hospices
offer incredible palliative care, that is, care to treat symptoms

rather than to cure a disease. But most hospices are small local charities without enough resources. And while most people would rather not end their lives in a hospital, 60 per cent of people do.

There isn't a one-size-fits-all answer for what makes a good death – it's a hugely personal and often upsetting decision. But death is also the only certainty in life, and allowing people to choose how they die, where they die, and who they want with them when they die is a start.

Take Action

▶ *Volunteer in a hospice* – and not just to raise funds for it. Whatever skills you have are likely to be useful. If you are a hairdresser or complementary therapist, for example, you might be able to provide treatments for hospice residents; if you are good at gardening, you may be able to help maintain the residents' grounds. Contact a local hospice and see which of your skills they might be able to tap.

▶ *Make a 'living will'.* A living will, or 'advance decision' as it is also known, is a legally binding document where you can give instructions in advance about the end-of-life treatment you would like to receive in case you lose the capacity to do so through a loss of mental competence or the ability to communicate. You should also let your friends, family, and doctors know about your wishes so that they can be carried out. A living will should be written down, dated, and witnessed. To be valid, it cannot ask for your life to be ended, force doctors to act against their professional judgement, or nominate someone else to decide treatment on your behalf. Suggested guidelines are available on the Age UK website, www.ageuk.org.uk.

▶ *Don't be afraid to talk about death and dying.* Share your plans and ideas about death with your close friends and family, especially if you may need help from them when the time comes.

Where to Get Started

Dignity in Dying is a national campaign group and membership organization that advocates greater choice over, control over, and access to services at the end of life.
181 Oxford Street
London W1D 2JT
Tel 020 7479 7730
www.dignityindying.org.uk

Help the Hospices supports providers and users of hospice care.
Hospice House
24–44 Britannia Street
London WC1X 9JG
Tel 020 7520 8200
www.helpthehospices.org.uk

Group engagement:
Learning to involve and inspire volunteers

Sam Bacon is a former non-profit community organizer and campaigns officer who has worked as a volunteer for Oxfam and Amnesty International, Campaigns Officer for The Industrial Alliance (a group representing local authorities in ex-coal mining/steel producing towns in the UK), Community Organizer for ESOP (Empowering and Strengthening Ohio's People) in the USA, and Policy Officer for Core Cities group (a group representing the eight largest cities outside London in England). Here are his top tips for engaging with volunteers.

- Know what you want your volunteers to accomplish and explain your aims and objectives to them.
- Don't take your volunteers' familiarity with the campaign for granted. Find out what they know, and speak at a level that matches their knowledge. Being involved heavily in a campaign often means you build up a large amount of knowledge, jargon, and acronyms that people new to the issue will not understand. Break it down for them and guide them through the issues so they can fully appreciate your point of view, and hopefully respond positively to it.
- Whenever you have meetings, ensure everyone that attends is asked to sign in, by providing their name, telephone number, home address, and email address.

Even if they don't come to your next meeting, you'll be able to follow up with them, if only to provide updates and information on what is happening with the campaign. It also means you can ask them to forward your emails to their contacts.

- Never let people leave your meetings without asking something of them and giving them an opportunity to do something to help. If you do need large numbers of people to achieve your campaign's objectives, then a good trick is to ask everyone to bring one extra person to the next meeting. It's a small task to bring a friend, but if everyone does it, the group doubles in size.

- Thanks to modern technology and social networking websites, there are more ways than ever before to spread the word about campaigns and events. Ask your volunteers to consider using Facebook or Twitter, or set up a campaign website or blog with an RSS feed that will deliver news straight to them. These tools can reach large numbers of people in very little time.

- For the overwhelming majority of campaigns, volunteers are the lifeblood for whatever you are trying to achieve. As such, it's crucial that you treat them like the prized commodities they are. The golden rule therefore is to be grateful. Try to ensure volunteers are treated in the best possible way. As well as thanking them this also means providing them with food and refreshments where possible, training them where necessary, and giving them as much responsibility as they want and can handle. If you are using your volunteers only for the mundane and thankless tasks, don't be surprised if they seem unenthused at the prospect of coming back to help you out.

- Most important, inspire your volunteers to share their own concern and passion for the campaign. Their personal stories can be a contagion, motivating them to do more and pulling other people to join you.

19

Support parents

According to Parentline Plus, there are over 24 million people in the UK who 'parent'. This includes mums and dads and grandparents, siblings, other relatives, friends, and carers who contribute to bringing up children. And whatever age or stage of you life you are at, parenting is a big deal and people need varying levels of support. After all, bringing children up to become emotionally and financially independent and to be 'good' people is not easy, especially when combined with having to earn a living at the same time.

In the past, parents could often turn to a close-knit community of relatives and neighbours for advice about everything from what food is most soothing for a teething baby to how to help a primary school student complete his or her homework without actually doing it for the child. In today's more mobile world, we may live far from our relatives or barely see our neighbours. So some parents must depend on more formal services, such as parenting classes, activities to prevent loneliness, financial help, and childcare.

Then of course there's the moral support that comes from living in a society that does not judge families that do not fit a typical two-parent mould. For instance, 'Don't judge my family' became a popular anti-Conservative slogan during the 2010 General Election, when the Conservative Party seemed to back traditional family units as the best possible way to have a family by promising them tax breaks. The slogan was inspired by an article published in *The Times* newspaper in the run-up to the election by 'Harry Potter' author JK Rowling, who described her time as a single parent and the challenges such families face.

It's often easy to judge parents for doing a bad job rather than help them to do a good one, but it's everyone's responsibility to do the latter. As the proverb says, it takes a village to raise a child.

Take Action

▶ *Don't judge*. Families come in all shapes and forms and all deserve support.

▶ *Help other families*. The cost of childcare is high, but perhaps you can help ease it in your community. Consider organizing babysitting circles with friends or local families so that you can take it in turns to have a night out, or join a skills swap and baby-sit in return for someone else helping you with gardening or another task.

▶ *Step in*. If you see children misbehaving, be it by dropping litter or bullying another child, explain to them why they need to stop. It is everybody's responsibility to teach right from wrong.

Where to Get Started

Parentline Plus offers help and support to people who parent and runs a free, twenty-four-hour-a-day helpline for parents as well as email and live chat services.
CAN Mezzanine
49–51 East Road
London N1 6AH
Tel 020 7553 3080
Helpline 0808 800 2222
www.parentlineplus.org.uk

Gingerbread seeks to improve the lives of single parent families. It also offers a free helpline.
255 Kentish Town Road
London NW5 2LX
Tel 020 74828 5400
Helpline 0808 802 0925
www.gingerbread.org.uk

The **Family and Parenting Institute** works for a family-friendly society which recognizes the whole family, values families in all their diversity, and promotes conditions which enable families to thrive. Each October it holds Parents' Week activities and fairs across the country.
430 Highgate Studios
53–79 Highgate Road
London NW5 1TL
Tel 020 7424 3460
www.familyandparenting.org

The **Daycare Trust** promotes high-quality, affordable childcare for all and runs an information line for parents giving advice on a range of issues including childcare options and how to get help with childcare costs.
2nd Floor, Novas Contemporary Urban Centre
73–81 Southwark Bridge Road
London SE1 0NQ
Tel 020 7940 7510
www.daycaretrust.org.uk

20

Talk about sex

We read about sex and see images of sex more than ever before, in magazines, on advertising hoardings, and on TV. Yet despite the prevalence of sexual images around us, many people see sex as something embarrassing to talk about, and ignorance abounds. Many people still believe myths, such as the idea you cannot get pregnant if you have sex while standing up or while in the shower. And there remain big gaps in people's knowledge and actions when it comes to preventing sexually transmitted diseases. Some surveys have even found that some people believe you can use cling film or chicken skin instead of a condom to prevent sexually transmitted diseases and pregnancy.

If we hope to limit the spread of sexual diseases, prevent unplanned pregnancies, and generally improve our sexual health – both physically and emotionally – we have to foster an environment in which people feel confident to have sex only when they want and to know the right form of contraception and protection to use for their situation. To do so, we need to educate ourselves, our partners, and our friends and even our parents and grandparents about sex, and this is just as important for men as it is for women.

What's more, while we may be more likely to feel pressured to have sex when we are younger, these issues apply at all ages. Reports from the UK's Health Protection Agency into sexually transmitted diseases show that people aged forty-five to sixty-four had the biggest rise in cases of syphilis, herpes, chlamydia, and genital warts between 2000 and 2009.

Take Action

▶ *Pick your protection.* If you are having sex or thinking about having it, think about contraception first. Discuss it with your partner and with a healthcare professional to find the method that suits you best. Regardless, always keep a stock of condoms and, if you're a woman, some emergency contraception (morning-after pills), at home, in case an accident happens.

▶ *Speak about sex with your friends.* Sex of course can be an intensely private thing, and you shouldn't feel compelled to talk about it. But speaking about sex with people you trust can reassure you that all kinds of feelings and activities are 'normal'. By the same token, avoid showing off about sex or making other people feel that their own sex lives, or lack of a sex life, is inadequate.

Where to Get Started

Owned and run by the charity YouthNet UK, **The Site** aims to be the first place all young adults turn to when they need support and guidance through life. It believes young people have the capacity to make their own decisions and choices, provided they have access to high-quality, impartial information and advice.
First Floor, 50 Featherstone Street
London EC1Y 8RT
Tel 020 7250 5716
www.thesite.org

The **FPA** (formerly Family Planning Association) provides straightforward information, advice, and support on all aspects of sexual health, sex, and relationships.
50 Featherstone Street
London EC1Y 8RT
Tel 020 7608 5240
Helpline 0845 122 8690
www.fpa.org.uk

Brook provides free and confidential sexual health advice and services specifically for people under twenty-five.
421 Highgate Studios
53–79 Highgate Road
London NW5 1TL
Tel 020 7284 6040
Helpline 0808 802 1234 (Monday to Friday, 9am–5pm)
www.brook.org.uk

Taking a lead:
The role of a charity trustee

Jessica Asato is Social Media Consultant and Founder of the Gareth Butler History Trust, which funds school history trips for disadvantaged young people. She is a Trustee of Brook (www.brook.org.uk), the UK's largest young people's sexual health charity, which has been providing advice and services for over forty years.

Q *What is a trustee?*

A A trustee of a charity is someone who is on the 'board' or 'governing body'. The trustees have responsibility for keeping a check on how the charity is run and providing it with strategic direction, and they are usually volunteers with a passion for the aims of that charity.

Q *How does somebody become a trustee of a charity?*

A Many vacancies for trustees are advertised in jobs pages of newspapers when they come up, but if you have a particular interest in supporting a particular charity as a trustee, simply send a covering letter and a CV asking if they have any vacancies. The National Council for Voluntary Organisations (NCVO) also keeps a list of trustee vacancies (www.ncvo-vol.org.uk), as do volunteering websites such as Do-it (www.do-it.org.uk).

The application process to become a trustee will depend on the organization. Usually it will involve filling in a form asking why you want to be a trustee and an interview or meeting with the organization you wish to join.

Q *Why did you choose Brook?*

A I saw a vacancy advertised for a trustee of Brook by accident. Having used Brook's services myself, I wanted to give something back to the organization and sent in an application. Brook is one of those unsung charities which contributes a huge amount to society, but hides its light under a bushel, and not a lot of people know about it.

Brook was established as a charity to support young unmarried women's access to contraception, and now it provides confidential advice and sexual health services for 100,000 people under twenty-five each year. Brook wants to see a demonstrable improvement in societal attitudes and intergenerational communication about sex, sexuality, and sexual health. We campaign to improve the quality and quantity of education and sexual health services in school, further education, and health and community settings. And most of all we want children and young people to be supported to develop the self-confidence, skills, and understanding they need to enjoy and take responsibility for their sexual lives, sexual health, and wellbeing.

Q *What does your role involve?*

A I am currently the Vice-Chair and a Trustee on the national board of Brook. The role involves providing support and challenge to the Chief Executive, helping to scrutinize decisions and strategy made by the senior management, and ensuring that Brook's objective of ensuring young people enjoy their sexuality without harm remains our number one focus.

Q *Is this the kind of thing anyone can get involved with?*

A Anyone who has passion for a charity and who understands the role of a trustee can get involved as I have. Given our charitable objectives, our board also has two young representatives to ensure the concerns of young people are the forefront of what Brook does. Other charities may operate differently, but most should welcome people from diverse backgrounds.

21

Prevent HIV and AIDS from being a death sentence

The fight against HIV and AIDS has come on apace in recent years, as the disease is better understood than ever before. Transmission of the HIV virus can be prevented by ensuring people practise safe sex and do not share needles, and the availability of anti-retroviral drugs means that people with HIV and AIDS can have a long life expectancy. So it's a modern-day tragedy that we now know so much about how the virus is transmitted and the disease is prevented and treated, yet people continue to become infected with HIV.

In the UK there are more people than ever before living with HIV, many of whom don't know they have it, in part because after successful public awareness campaigns in the 1980s and 1990s, the twenty-first century has seen complacency grow about the risks.

There is also a schism in how people with HIV and AIDS are treated in the developing world compared to those in developed countries. After the international community put pressure on pharmaceutical companies, anti-retroviral drugs became available in these countries for a minimal price. Though several million people there had received these treatments by 2010, there is a shortfall; less than half of people with HIV in sub-Saharan Africa, for instance, had access to them. There is also still ignorance, including amongst politicians, about how the virus can be transmitted.

Short-term financial aid is not the solution, because to treat the disease there needs to be long-term commitment to funding anti-retroviral drugs. If treatment stops, people die; it's as simple as that. Yet governments have not committed to this kind of aid. Consequently, people with HIV and AIDS in the developing world have a death sentence hanging over them.

So the fight against HIV and AIDS is two-fold. In developed countries it requires better public information campaigns and more education about how the disease spreads and the risks of infection, and in developing countries it requires educating leaders, promising long-term funding for treatment, finding the money to train more healthcare professionals where they are needed most, and building the health infrastructure necessary to teach people about preventing the spread of the disease. With these efforts, we could potentially eradicate the disease altogether.

Take Action

▶ *Challenge people who say HIV/AIDS is no longer an issue.* Continued ignorance only risks that more people will be infected.

▶ *Get tested.* If you have had unsafe sex or shared needles for drug use, it is important to get tested; early treatment is vital to enjoying a long life. Most hospitals have special units, called genitourinary medicine (GUM) clinics, which will test you, and many organizations offer free, anonymous tests.

▶ *Spread the word.* Hold an HIV awareness event at your school, youth club, or community organization. Lesson plans for teachers are available on the Terrence Higgins Trust website, where you can also find lots of ideas for combining an awareness event with fundraising.

Where to Get Started

AVERT is an international charity, based in the UK, working to avert HIV and AIDS worldwide, through education, treatment, and care.
4 Brighton Road
Horsham
West Sussex RH13 5BA
www.avert.org

The **Terrence Higgins Trust** is the largest HIV and sexual health charity in the UK. It seeks to empower everyone living with HIV in the UK to maximize their health and wellbeing by working to ensure the best possible HIV treatment and support services are available. It also leads public and political support for HIV and sexual health issues

and campaigns to eradicate stigma and discrimination around HIV/AIDS.
314–320 Gray's Inn Road
London WC1Z 8DP
Tel 020 7812 1600
Helpline 0845 1221 200
www.tht.org.uk

The **National AIDS Trust** (NAT) is dedicated to transforming society's response to HIV by providing expert advice and practical resources those infected with the virus.
New City Cloisters
196 Old Street
London EC1V 9FR
Tel 020 7814 6767
www.nat.org.uk

22

Eradicate preventable diseases

There are many diseases that we know how to prevent or eradicate, or for which we have found treatments that lessen their long-term impact, but for reasons of poverty, ignorance, or logistics we don't always manage to succeed in doing so.

Vaccinations, for example, are a safe and effective way of preventing many diseases, including measles. Yet according to the World Health Organization there were 164,000 measles deaths globally in 2008 – nearly 450 deaths every day, or eighteen deaths every hour. There are also effective vaccinations for polio, diphtheria, and tuberculosis. Malaria nets are a huge help in preventing malaria, one of the world's deadliest diseases. Further, diseases such as measles and pneumonia are often associated with poverty.

To truly eradicate preventable diseases, we need effective education programmes that ensure people know how diseases spread and how they can avoid them as well as money to support the proper training of health professionals, universal access to pharmaceutical treatments, and an end to malnutrition and unsanitary living conditions which make it easier for diseases to spread from person to person.

Ironically, because of the effectiveness of immunization programmes in the West, there is a risk that people will stop having their children vaccinated because they assume some diseases are no longer a problem. This trend gained some support due to fears, caused by misinformation from Dr Andrew Wakefield that has since been widely discredited by numerous scientific studies, that there might be a link between the Measles, Mumps, and Rubella (MMR) vaccination and rising rates of autism. Unfortunately, in some parts of the UK and the USA, the movement against MMR and other vaccinations means that there is no longer a 'herd immunity', in which people are protected when everybody acts responsibly and get immunized, and diseases we thought we had under control are starting to show up again.

Given that we have the knowledge to fight so many preventable diseases, and even to eradicate some of them, it is a huge waste of science and of life to not so.

Take Action

▶ *Take your doctor's advice*. Follow government-issued medical guidelines when it comes to vaccinations and disease prevention for yourself and your children. Not doing so doesn't just endanger your life or your child's life, but the lives of everyone around you.

▶ *Fight poverty*. Diseases thrive in communities that do not have proper access to food and sanitation. Your support for charities and organizations that fight poverty may do as much to prevent diseases as lobbying for cheaper drugs and treatments.

Where to Get Started

The **World Health Organization** (WHO) is the directing and coordinating authority for health within the United Nations system and provides a variety of research and statistics on its website that can be used to better understand preventable diseases.
Avenue Appia 20
1211 Geneva 27
Switzerland
Tel + 41 22 791 21 11

The **Bill and Melinda Gates Foundation** operates a Global Health Program to harness advances in science and technology to save lives in poor countries and to invest in research and development of new interventions, such as vaccines, drugs, and diagnostics.
PO Box 23350
Seattle, WA 98102
USA
Tel +1 206 709 3100
info@gatesfoundation.org

23

Give all women choice over abortion

Many of us are lucky enough to live in a society in which we can access safe, legal abortion: no backstreet abortionists or do-it-yourself attempts that maim and sometimes kill women. But there is a mistaken belief that women in the UK have 'abortion on demand'. Instead, women who have made the difficult decision to have an abortion are forced to jump through a series of bureaucratic hoops. These include getting the written permission of two doctors, a policy which goes against the principle of 'informed consent' that applies to most clinical practice. This means a woman cannot request an abortion for herself; she has to persuade two separate doctors to agree that she should have one based on restrictive legal criteria.

But a significant group of women in the UK are excluded from even this level of access to abortion. Though women in England, Scotland, and Wales are entitled to a legal, safe abortion on the NHS, a woman in Northern Ireland is not, even if her pregnancy is the result of rape or incest. To get an abortion, she has to find a clinic elsewhere in the UK or Europe and pay about £2000 for the procedure. She has to make all the arrangements herself, including where to stay and, if she already has children, arranging childcare for them. Since 1967, 80,000 women have travelled from Northern Ireland to seek access to a safe abortion.

Choosing to have an abortion is hard for a woman, but once her decision has been made then getting one shouldn't be even harder for her. After all, 83 per cent of people in Britain support a woman's right to choose and one in three women will need an abortion at some point in their lives. If that doesn't persuade you, then the knowledge that making access to abortion harder doesn't stop abortion should; all restricted access does is make desperate women put themselves in danger to get the medical help they need.

Take Action

▶ *Find out what is going on in your local school.* Anti-abortion groups are allowed into schools across the country to present their arguments to teenagers, often in Religious Education classes or as part of lessons on rights or ethics. You can make a difference by contacting local schools and making sure young people in your area receive accurate, objective information on pregnancy, sexual health, and abortion.

▶ *Challenge abortion myths.* There is no evidence to support the assertion that women are careless about using contraception because abortion is available. There is no link between abortion and infertility, miscarriage, or stillbirth, and women who have had abortions are at no greater risk of breast cancer than those who have not.

▶ *Don't stigmatize abortion* – and do speak openly about it. Having an abortion is always a hard decision to make but we only make it harder if people feel they must keep it a secret.

Where to Get Started

Marie Stopes International runs sexual health clinics in the UK and around the world, including safe, supportive, and non-judgmental advice and help on abortion.
Tel 020 7636 6200
Helpline 0845 300 8090
www.mariestopes.org.uk

Abortion Rights campaigns to defend and extend women's rights and access to safe, legal abortion.
18 Ashwin Street
London E8 3DL
Tel 020 7923 9792
www.abortionrights.org.uk

Group action:
Sharing common experiences with people who can change things

Geraldine Holden is Content Editor at Mumsnet, a parenting website and internet forum (www.mumsnet.com). One of the site's campaigns is for a Miscarriage Standard Code of Practice, which would set guidelines for how to treat women who are experiencing a miscarriage. The site is monitored by many politicians to test parents' reactions to policies. In fact, the 2010 UK General Election was dubbed 'The Mumsnet Election' by the press as it was thought that parent voters would determine the outcome.

Q *How did the miscarriage campaign start?*

A A lot of Mumsnet contributors had, over time, started threads about how upset they were at the type of care they received after having a miscarriage; it became a recurring theme. Alan Johnson, who was Secretary of State for Health at the time, came on to Mumsnet for a webchat. He was one of the first high-profile politicians to come on the site.

During the webchat Alan Johnson asked people for concrete things they thought could be improved or that they were upset by and lots of people mentioned miscarriage care. He said he would go away and look at it. So afterwards we came up with a ten-point plan based on ideas from our users. They were suggestions for improving the care of women who had had miscarriages and included things like the medicalized language that is used – which people find very upsetting – or being put on wards where other women are in labour.

Q *What did you do with the ten-point plan?*

A We sent the plan to Alan Johnson; to the relevant departments in Scotland, Wales, and Northern Ireland; to chief nurses; to anyone who would have a say or be involved in developing policy. There was a bit of a lull and Mumsnetters kept asking what was happening with it. And then Prime Minister Gordon Brown came on Mumsnet to do a webchat and he promised to go away and find out what was happening on the plan.

Q *Did the Prime Minister do anything about it?*

A Well, after Brown's webchat a Mumsnet representative, along with lots of other interested parties, was invited to a meeting at the Department of Health. There, action points were agreed. It was the first time we'd been invited to this kind of meeting.

There is a feeling that this is an area where Mumsnet will tangibly feed an improvement in policy and in care. There's been a change of government since then, so we're keeping the pressure on, and trying to get a meeting with the current secretary of state for health.

24

End the stigma of mental health issues

Mental health is one of those catch-all phrases that means different things to different people. For some the words 'mental health issues' immediately registers as depression; for others it calls up self-harm, eating disorders, contemplations of suicide, hearing voices. But whatever it means to you, it often comes with a stigma attached. People are wary of talking about any mental health issues they may be facing for fear of being labelled, being judged, or ruining employment prospects.

Almost as difficult is defining what is meant by having 'good mental health'. Being in good mental health means you are able to cope with life and all its ups and downs, make the most of your potential, and play a full role in your family and community. When you aren't in good mental health, one or all of these strands will likely start to fray.

One in four people will suffer from a mental health issue each year. So while you may not be affected directly, you are very likely to know someone who is. But because mental health often doesn't have a physical symptom, you might not be able to spot someone's issue. And people suffering from a mental health issue often don't feel able to seek help or talk to their families or friends, because the term is stigmatized. We need to end this stigma and recognize that mental health issues, like physical health issues, need understanding, treatment, and support.

Take Action

▶ *Get positive.* The Time to Change website provides ideas for how to hold an event promoting positive mental health for your local school or community group.

▶ *Share your story.* By talking openly about your own mental health and emotions, it makes it easier for others to do so.

▶ *Be available.* Help people you know by listening when and if they decide they would like to talk about their problems with mental health. Don't be judgemental. Instead, ask them what help, if any, they would like to get from you.

Where to Get Started

Rethink works to help everyone affected by severe mental illness recover a better quality of life.
15th Floor, 89 Albert Embankment
London SE1 7TP
Tel 0845 456 0455
Helpline 020 7840 3188
(Monday–Friday, 10am–2pm) or
advice@rethink.org
www.rethink.org

YoungMinds is committed to improving the emotional wellbeing and mental health of children and young people and to empowering their parents and carers.

48–50 St John Street
London EC1M 4DG
Tel 020 7336 8445
www.youngminds.org.uk

Time to Change is a collaborate programme of projects organized by Rethink and Mind. Their projects all aim to end mental health discrimination.
15–19 Broadway
London E15 4BQ
Tel 020 8215 2357
www.time-to-change.org.uk

Help people you know who may have a mental health issue

- Be there to talk and listen.
- If someone talks to you, don't brush it off, acknowledge his or her problem and let the person know you're there for him or her.
- Make time to stay in touch. Call, visit, or invite your friend round; carry on with whatever you normally do.
- Ask the person how you can help; people will want support at different times in different ways.
- Keep in mind that having a mental health issue is just one part of the person. People don't want to be defined by it.
- Think about the words you use. Words like nutter, crazy, and psycho can hurt.

Adapted and reproduced with permission from the Time to Change website, www.time-to-change.org.uk.

The personal and the political:
Transforming private issues into public policies

Michelle Smith is a member of the campaigns and policy team at Rethink (www.rethink.org), a mental health membership charity with a focus on the needs of people affected by severe mental illness. She faces the hard task of having to get decision makers to respond to a subject many people don't want to talk about.

Q *Other than helping people they already know, how can a person get involved in helping people affected by a mental health issue?*

A At Rethink, we encourage people to become members (we offer a pay-what-you-can membership) and to sign up to our campaigner mailings. Our activists have access to a range of opportunities for getting involved, whether it's taking part in a policy focus group or joining us in a mass lobby of Parliament. Online campaigning is also a really easy way to make a difference – many of our successful campaigns have used e-campaigns at some point to demonstrate the weight of the issue.

Q *Do you have to become a full-time campaigner to make a difference?*

A There are so many different ways to get involved, some of which are really low effort if you're strapped for time: sending a ready-made email to your local politicians through our regular e-campaigns, meeting with your MP in Parliament or in the surgery he or she holds in your constituency to meet with local people who want to raise concerns. Or you can take part in one-off events or tell us about your experiences so that we can go to decision makers at a national level with credible evidence to back up our case. All of these activities help to create momentum around mental health issues and challenge stigma.

Q *What campaigning tools have worked best for you?*

A If it's simply about raising profile and awareness, local events can be really powerful, especially if you get the media involved. Engaging your MP is great if it's a national issue; whether you get your MP to write a letter to a Cabinet minister or ask questions about the issue in Parliament, that can help with a local campaign. The most important thing is identifying what needs to change, and who has the power to change it.

Q *What are you campaigning on now?*

A At Rethink we are busy making the case to the government to protect frontline mental health services. Because mental illness is still such a stigmatized area, these services are often seen as a soft option for cuts in hard times, and people who use them might not have the confidence to shout about them. Essentially, we need everyone to join the movement in making mental health a priority issue. Even though we rarely talk about it, we all know someone who has experienced a mental health problem, be it anxiety, depression, or psychosis. One in four people will experience a problem at some point – mental health should be a mainstream issue.

25

Be disability aware

Perhaps you have, or know someone with, a disability. Or perhaps you have experienced the difficulties of having an injury that has restricted your mobility – for example being on crutches. If not, it's easy not to realize the issues involved for a person with a disability in doing what you think of as simple, everyday activities. Tasks such as getting dressed, using the toilet, getting on a bus, or going to the shops can be challenging. So can things many of us take for granted, such as whether you can get into a restaurant or take holiday accommodation without checking that the building is accessible, or whether you can get information or advice without spending time finding a publication in a format you can access. For people with disabilities, these are all things they must think about every day.

And then there are tasks such as finding a job, an area in which disabled people often face unfair treatment. Although the passage of the Disability Discrimination Act in 1995 and the Equality Act in 2010 promote civil rights for disabled people and protect them from discrimination, life is still made harder for people with a disability than it could be.

For these reasons, disability shouldn't simply be seen as a challenge; it should be seen as a human rights issue. It's about facing physical, social, and attitudinal barriers every day. It's about equality and freedom, about being able to make your own decisions in life,

We all need to become disability aware. We need to recognize that not all disabilities are physically obvious, to ensure that unnecessary barriers to access are removed, and to encourage people to explain their needs, and to work to accommodate those needs wherever possible.

Take Action

▶ *Offer support.* Many disability organizations need volunteers for activities, ranging from driving people to organizing activities to advising people on their rights.

▶ *Be disability aware in your community.* If you are organizing an event, make sure it is held in a building that is accessible to people with a disability. Ensure that there are accessible toilets and parking nearby reserved for people with a disability. If a restaurant, shop, theatre, or other service has particularly good access for people with a disability, praise them for it and let others know through online reviews and recommendations. Conversely, where access is poor, make sure people know about that, too.

▶ *Be disability aware in your workplace.* If you are an employer, think about how any job vacancy you have can be made as accessible as possible, and flag up the vacancy with organizations that can disseminate the opportunity to people with a disability.

Where to Get Started

Disability Alliance works to relieve the poverty and improve the living standards of disabled people.
Universal House
88–94 Wentworth Street
London E1 7SA
Tel 020 7247 8776
www.disabilityalliance.org

Disability Awareness in Action is an international disability and human rights network whose mission is to provide information and evidence to support disabled people in their own actions to secure their rights. It also publishes a monthly e-newsletter, 'Our Rights'.

46 The Parklands
Hullavington
Wiltshire SN14 6DL
www.daa.org.uk

Leonard Cheshire Disability exists to change attitudes to disability and to serve people with a disability around the world. Its main activity in the UK is the provision of services in support including care homes, supported living, domiciliary support, day services, resource centres, rehabilitation, respite care, personal support, and training and assistance for those looking for work.
66 South Lambeth Road
London SW8 1RL
Tel 020 3242 0200
www.lcdisability.org

26

Promote 'unsexy' causes

Some illnesses and health issues have captured the public's imagination. This is great – being a 'popular' cause means extra funding, research, and awareness. For example, breast cancer has gained a very high profile when it comes to fundraising and awareness. In the USA, more than a million people participate each year in local Race for the Cure events. Pink ribbons, hats, T-shirts, and other goods are sold in support of breast cancer research and used to encourage women to examine their breasts monthly and receive regular mammograms later in life. The fashion industry has embraced the cause, with a special 'Fashion Targets Breast Cancer' range. Famous landmarks, from Sydney's Harbour Bridge to Niagara Falls and from Constantine's Arch in Rome to the White House in Washington, DC, have been bathed in pink lights to publicize the issue.

None of this should be begrudged – breast cancer is an important health issue and it's excellent that so much notice is taken of it. But we need to ensure we don't let less popular causes fall by the wayside. It is hard to imagine our intestines having the same appeal as breasts, or a brown ribbon campaign taking off, yet bowel cancer is the UK's second biggest cancer killer.

We need to increase funding, research, and awareness for lots of diseases, so seek out ways to help whatever illnesses or causes you may know about, especially if they don't get much publicity at the moment. This doesn't just include cancers, of course, but the many other diseases that affect our health and mortality.

Supporting less trendy causes is just as important as supporting the better known ones, and yours may be the only support these causes get.

Take Action

▶ *Make it personal*. If you have a connection to an illness – perhaps a friend or relative has it – look up any support groups or campaigning organizations working in this area and see what help they need, from fundraising to volunteering in the office a few hours a week.

▶ *Talk to people*. If people have never heard of an illness they are unlikely to do anything to contribute to fundraising for research on it. You can also help to raise raise awareness about preventing the disease by explaining how to spot its symptoms early.

Breast cancer isn't the only cancer

The nineteen most common causes of death from cancer in the UK, in descending order, are: lung, colorectal, breast, prostate, oesophagus, stomach, bladder, non-Hodgkin lymphoma, ovary, all leukaemias, kidney, brain with central nervous system, liver, multiple myeloma, mesothelioma, malignant melanoma, oral, uterus, and bone and connective tissue.

Source: Cancer Research UK. Data for 2008.

Selling your story: How to get media attention

Keiron Pim is a feature writer for the *Eastern Daily Press* (EDP), a newspaper based in East Anglia. His work has covered several campaigns in the region, helping to raise awareness of local issues and raise funds for local projects.

Q *How can campaigners get their issue into their local media?*

A It might sound obvious, but to attract the attention of a journalist on a regional paper, you'll need a strong local angle. Explain how your issue relates to people living in that newspaper's circulation area. Also think about having a 'hook' – something topical that makes the campaign appear urgent, such as an aim to reach a certain target by a certain date or a reason you are campaigning on an issue at this point in time (such as an anniversary). Of course, your target needs to be achievable, since newspapers want to cover a success story – and won't want to lend their names to a campaign that never reaches its goal.

Q *When should the media be contacted? Is it important that your issue is 'breaking news' in order to get coverage?*

A Think about the amount of notice you're giving journalists of any events you're planning to hold. Don't tell them the same day or the day before. A few days' notice is best; more is better if you're dealing with a features desk, as they tend to work to longer deadlines and plan their editorial content further in advance than the news desk.

Q *Is it important to have stunts and awareness days or is a strong story enough?*

A Awareness days are no good without a strong issue behind them, but if that's in place I think they can help catch a journalist's attention by giving the issue a hook. There are a lot of strong stories out there that deserve coverage so there's no harm in making sure that yours stands out. Plenty of successful campaigns over the years have also benefited from having an easily recognizable accessory people can wear, whether it's a Make Poverty History wristband or a pink ribbon for breast cancer awareness or a plastic red nose for Comic Relief. If you come up with something similar, that might help catch a journalist's attention too.

Q *Are pictures important?*

A Very important. It can be annoying to receive an interesting sounding press release but find that there are no pictures provided. At the very least, you should be able to offer the names of some local people who have agreed to act as case studies and have their picture taken by one of the newspaper's photographers.

If you do send photographs, be sure to have them available at a high enough resolution for reproduction in the newspaper. For instance, we ask for JPEG files of at least 500KB, and preferably over 1MB, though each publication will have its own requirement. Bear in mind also that papers are increasingly looking to have something different to offer on their websites, so you might also consider offering video footage that gives a flavour of your campaign, say, a personal message delivered by a celebrity who you have on board as a supporter of the campaign interspersed with film illustrating the issue.

Q *Do you have a favourite campaign or issue that has received lots of media coverage?*

A I worked with a local charity with a view to my newspaper supporting a campaign to raise money for them to build a purpose-built, eco-friendly new office. The charity is called Nelson's Journey and it offers bereavement services to children in Norfolk who have lost a close family member. It was an ideal campaign for us because it's a very worthwhile charity that is based in and helps people in our region; the campaign has a certain 'wow factor' in the form of a striking new eco-build office that will be substantially constructed from straw bales and mud; they have a clear and achievable target for the campaign; and there are plenty of local case studies in place. There was also potential for some good stunts to raise awareness. The campaign is called the Smiles Campaign, with a logo of a smile, and so they are looking into having aerial photographs of Norfolk taken showing groups of people standing in the form of a smile. This would provide eye-catching photography, a chance for our readers to get involved, and it would reinforce the campaign's logo.

Down to basics: Press releases

The purpose of a press release is to give journalists information about a campaign or event that is going to happen or has happened, so that they can consider including it in their publication or programme. Journalists receive many press releases every day, so it can sometimes be more helpful to make personal contact with journalists you already have a relationship with; however, even in that case, it is useful to have a press release to email them if they tell you they are interested, so they have all the necessary information about your campaign or event in one place. The main components of a press release are:

- The date. Journalists need to be able to know when the press release was issued, so it's clear that the information they have is current.
- Any embargo. An embargo is the earliest the information can be made public. If you use an embargo you should give a date and time for when journalists can report on your release's contents. An embargo should only be used in rare situations – for example, when a protest is a secret and meant to take people by surprise. The more flexibility journalists have, the more likely they are to be able to use the information or report on it.
- A catchy headline explaining what the press release is about. Don't use puns or try to be clever – many

journalists will get no further than reading your head-line, so use it to make your news clear.

- A first line explaining what is happening. Think of this as the 'five Ws' – the first line should explain who, what, why, where, and when.
- Another sentence or two explaining the issue in a little more detail.
- A quotation from the organizer and, if possible, from somebody with a personal take on the subject, such as one of the people you are trying to help.
- Any extra information, including famous supporters, key dates that might help journalists conduct their reporting, or facts and figures they might want to cite in their stories.
- Whether you have any pictures available that can be published, and whether you or any of your supporters are available for interview.
- Your contact details, including a mobile phone number, so that any journalists wanting to cover the story can contact you for more information.
- Some press releases include an extra 'Notes for Editors' section at the bottom. This might give background information on your campaign that journalists may find helpful but that isn't vital to the specific story you are presenting in the release.

27

Call for more public toilets

For many of us, needing the toilet when you are out and about is just a nuisance. For others, it can be a serious impediment to a normal life. If you need the toilet regularly, perhaps because you are pregnant, old, or have a medical condition, not having easy access to cheap or free toilet facilities can make you less willing to leave the house in case you are caught short, even to do something simple like go to the shops or stroll around the park. In fact, Help the Aged (now part of Age UK) estimates that 3.5 million people suffer from urinary incontinence in the UK. They also report that 78 per cent of people say their local public toilets are not open when they need them. This means a lot of worry for a lot of people.

What's more, the lack of toilet facilities can mean some people decide to spend a penny in the street instead, leaving an unpleasant smell and a public health risk. All local authorities should be compelled to provide adequate public toilets, and shops and businesses should be encouraged to let the public use theirs.

Take Action

▶ *Spend several pennies.* Ask local shops and restaurants to display a sign allowing the public to use their loo – and mention that this passing trade is likely to earn them more money, too. Some local authorities already pay businesses a small fee to display a small sign letting people know that they can use their facilities.

▶ *Plan ahead*. If there are new shopping centres or bus or train stations in the works, look up the plans and write to the developers and your local council asking that adequate public toilet facilities be included.

▶ *Demand more toilets*. Write to your local authority and local councillors asking for more public toilets in your area. And where public toilets already exist, write to your local authority asking for longer opening hours and security measures to ensure they are safe.

Where to Get Started

Keep Britain Tidy is an environmental and anti-litter charity. Its work includes campaigning for more public toilets.
Elizabeth House
The Pier
Wigan WN3 4EX
Tel 01942 612 621
www.keepbritaintidy.org

Persuading the decision makers: How to get politicians' attention

Richard Messingham has worked for MPs in Westminster, and in political affairs for a number of charities and campaign groups. He currently works as Public Affairs Adviser to a professional membership body, and offers these ideas for getting politicians and their staff to pay attention to your campaign.

How to write an effective letter to a decision maker

Writing a letter or an email is probably the most common way for individuals to make contact with a decision maker. In many instances you will be contacting your MP or councillor, in order to put forward a point of view or to ask him or her to do something. Decision makers can include anyone in a position of power or responsibility, for example the chair of a local NHS Trust, a school governor, or the mayor of London. To find out who your elected representatives are, enter your postcode into the Write to Them website (www.writetothem.com). When making contact with a decision maker, you need to remember the following three key elements of any communication:

1. *Make sure you are contacting the right person.* Is this the right person to write to? For example should you be contacting your local councillor rather than your MP? If it is a local issue, such as the closure of a swimming pool

or a library, then perhaps your local councillor is more appropriate. However, whilst most MPs do not themselves make major decisions, they will be able to write on your behalf to the relevant Cabinet minister, and lend their support to your case – though only if they agree with you, of course.

2. *Keep to the point, and make just a couple of key points.* Any decision maker will have limited time and resources, and will have many other groups and individuals contacting him or her about a number of other issues. Whilst your issue is important to you, it will not always be so to the decision maker. Keep any letter or email short, including just a couple of key issues; for a letter, always keep to one side of A4. You can provide more information at a meeting or in another letter.

3. *Give him or her something to do.* The only point of writing to decision makers is to ask them to do something. Five pages of rant may help you get something off your chest, but it will achieve nothing. Always think about what you want the person to do. This will depend on who you are writing to and what he or she can practically achieve. If you are asking a decision maker to write to someone else, such as the prime minister, to advocate on your behalf, then ask him or her to send back any response, so you know what is happening with your issue. Sometimes requesting and securing a meeting is the best outcome of a letter.

Meeting a decision maker

Decision makers are generally busy people, and may be only able to meet you for ten minutes, perhaps at one of their weekly surgeries in your local area. If you have managed to secure a meeting, you should remember these key points:

1. *Be on time and presentable.* Remember that time is scarce, and that if you're meeting senior decision makers, you should be smartly dressed.

2. *Prepare a list of issues and stick to them.* Think through in advance what you want to raise, keeping to the key points. If you have any extra information you want to give to the decision maker, such as a report or image, then bring it along and bring enough copies. Be prepared for the person you're meeting to only to read this information after the meeting.

3. *Give the decision maker something to do.* For the meeting to have a purpose, you must ask the person to do something. This could be as simple as asking him or her to vote against a bill or to give support to a local campaign or initiative. After the meeting, make sure you follow up with a note of thanks, and reiterate the key points you made and what you'd like the person to do.

28

Insist on equal representation

Politics is not only about the decisions made, but the messages sent out. If all of the decision makers are middle-class white men then this sends a message to other people in society that they aren't worthy to be in important roles, making important decisions. It also means the experiences of those in power are narrow and don't reflect the experiences of all the people they serve and represent. For this reason, we need more women, more ethnic minorities, and more people from all types of community and all types of financial and class background, in Parliament and other positions of power.

What's more, we have to ensure that once in positions of power, these representatives from diverse walks of life are taken seriously. This involves not letting people get away with disparaging comments about women or minorities in public life, even if the comments are 'coded' – that 'she's okay but' and 'he's okay but' culture. These go something like 'she's okay but she's like a school teacher' (meaning she's hectoring) or 'he's okay but he owns a caravan' (meaning he's unstable) or 'she's okay but she wears funny shoes' (meaning she's too liberal) or 'he's okay but he always talks about the mosque' (meaning he's too 'ethnic'). These sorts of comment, which can sometimes appear in news and opinion articles, serve to undermine the authority of women and minorities in Parliament and local councils, and to discourage people like them from giving their own opinions or running for office.

I was on the point of giving up. I was fed up going to these selections and not getting it because I didn't have a willy

EMILY THORNBERRY, MEMBER OF PARLIAMENT (ISLINGTON SOUTH)

Take Action

▶ *Try not to make assumptions.* Don't expect all MPs to be white men, don't refer to politicians by the default 'him', and encourage people from all backgrounds that they can put themselves forward for selection and election.

▶ *Stand for election yourself.* The usual route to do this is through a political party. Choose which one best reflects your values and join it.

▶ *Watch the language.* When journalists or columnists use sexist, racist, or homophobic language about a politician, write a letter of complaint to them and to their editor – public opinion matters.

Where to Get Started

The **Electoral Commission** has advice on standing for election, registering political parties, and understanding election rules.
Trevelyan House
Great Peter Street
London SW1P 2HW
Tel 020 7271 0500
www.electoralcommission.org.uk

The **Fawcett Society** campaigns for equality between men and women in the UK and collects and shares lots of information on female political representation.
1–3 Berry Street
London EC1V 0AA
Tel 020 7253 2598
www.fawcettsociety.org.uk

The **Public Appointments** website provides details of current vacancies on the boards of UK public bodies and on a range of government committees.
publicappointments.cabinetoffice.gov.uk

Making the most of your representative:
How to get your MP's help

Kerry McCarthy has been Member of Parliament for Bristol East since 2005.

Q *What issues can people contact their MP about?*

A Anything. Individuals have come to me for help with issues such as asylum and immigration, housing, benefits, child support agency, and so on. I can also help with what I call issue-based case-work, where it's something that affects more than the individual who first contacts me, as with planning, traffic and parking, school closures, or youth facilities. I help community groups who need funding and local businesses who want me to lobby on their behalf. I also do policy work, where someone wants to make his or her views known to me or wants to ask me my views on an issue.

Q *What makes you likely to take people seriously if they approach you about an issue?*

A I get absolutely bombarded with lobbying material, and there are only a handful of topics that make it into my reading tray – but if it has a local connection, then I will definitely be interested. It helps if I have a pre-existing relationship with an organization or if it's an issue I already know a bit about. For example, I've done a lot of work on child poverty and know all the parliamentary officers of the main organizations working on it.

It also helps if people know what they actually want from me – it's amazing how many people ask for a meeting, and they just talk round an issue, or bombard me with information. At the end of the day an MP wants to know what he or she can do to help, such as raising an issue with a minister or in Parliament. The more specific the 'ask' the better. And keep it simple; some MPs do become absolute experts on their subjects, but most of us are trying to juggle 101 different things and whilst we want to help, we physically and mentally can't handle everything that comes our way.

Q *Who can't you help?*

A I try not to get involved in commercial disputes. And sometimes people contact me because they can't afford a lawyer, and if they really do need a lawyer I have to tell them that.

Q *Can you give an example of a successful campaign you've been involved with?*

A An example would be child poverty. One year I got more than a hundred Labour MPs to sign a letter to the chancellor of the exchequer ahead of the budget, which was published in the *Observer* – and we did get more funding for the issue. That was partly about making a good case, that is, identifying the problem, and what action was needed to tackle it; it was partly about showing the strength of support for it; and it was also about being realistic in what we were asking for.

Q *Any tips for people who care strongly about an issue and want to start campaigning on it?*

A Be clear about what you want. It's not enough to be highlighting that something is terrible, you need to know what the 'ask' is. You also need to know who to target, For example, if you want more youth facilities, the MP can support this but it's likely to be the council that provides them, so find out who your councillors are, how the council works, and where the money is. Some campaigns are simply about raising awareness of an issue which you feel has been neglected, but to actually make progress you need some demands, even if it's just to get a politician to sign up in support of your campaign and thus demonstrate you've got some support from key figures.

29

Campaign for gay equality

Gay rights have come a long way. It's hard to believe that in the UK you could still be sacked for being gay right up until 2003, or that the age of consent was not equalized until 2001. You were barred from joining any of the armed forces if you were gay up until 1999. And if you attended school in the fifteen years between 1988 and 2003, the law criminalized any staff who 'promoted' homosexuality, so you probably wouldn't have heard much positive discussion of gay lives.

But despite these advances, gay people are not always treated equally. Homophobic bullying is endemic in schools, homophobic hate crime is rife in some towns and villages, and some wedding venues refuse to conduct civil partnership ceremonies. In response, Stonewall, a charity that campaigns for lesbian, gay, and bisexual equality, recently staged a poster campaign with the simple message: 'Some people are gay. Get over it.' That's precisely what this issue is about.

> *At Stonewall, we don't campaign for "gay rights". We campaign for gay equality. The crucial difference is, all of our campaigning focuses on lesbian, gay, and bisexual people being treated fairly and in exactly the same way as everybody else rather than asking for any special extra "rights"*
>
> GAY EQUALITY CAMPAIGNER

Take Action

▶ *Demand answers*. Write to your old school – or your child's school – and ask what it's doing to tackle homophobic bullying.

▶ *Take responsibility*. Become a governor at your local school – they play a vital role in setting policy – and ensure that the school takes a zero-tolerance approach to homophobic bullying. Contact your local school to ask if there are any vacancies.

▶ *Be proud*. Display 'Some People Are Gay. Get Over It!' posters, postcards, or stickers – available from Stonewall – in your youth club, community centre, school, or meeting place.

Where to Get Started

Stonewall was founded after the passage of Section 28 of the Local Government Act 1988, which was designed to prevent 'promotion' of homosexuality – including acceptance of it – in schools. It aims to prevent similar attacks on lesbians, gay men, and bisexuals from ever occurring again.
Tower Building
York Road
London SE1 7NX
Tel 0800 050 2020
www.stonewall.org.uk

The **Queer Youth Network** campaigns for equal rights for lesbian, gay, bisexual, and transgendered (LGBT) people and provides support to young people who are 'coming out' or who are a target of homophobia.
49–51 Sidney Street
Manchester M1 7HB
Tel 0208 123 6958
www.queeryouth.org.uk

Starting something:
How campaigns can quickly grow beyond your control

Richard Lane is Events and Fundraising Officer of LGBT Labour, the Lesbian, Gay, Bisexual and Transgender section of the Labour Party. When the group experienced homophobia in a London pub, members put their experiences on the internet and experienced a massive amount of support.

Q *Tell me about the incident at the pub.*

A In June 2010 LGBT Labour held its Annual General Meeting in Westminster, London. It was on a Saturday afternoon and afterwards I had organized for everyone there to head to a nearby pub – there were about fifty of us. I had pre-booked this and reserved an area with the pub, and when we got there we put up the LGBT Labour banner in our reserved area and began to enjoy the rest of the afternoon. We had been in the pub for about two hours with no problem when a customer complained loudly about our presence in the bar. This began a heated discussion between the customer and a number of our members, who took objection to his comments against lesbian and gay people.

Our members quickly left the confrontation to a member of staff, who went over to speak to the customer to establish what the problem was. Shortly afterwards the member of staff approached me and forcefully asked for me to take down our banner, which had been standing in our reserved area for almost two hours. When I asked him what the problem seemed to be, he began muttering that they didn't want 'that sort of thing' in the pub and that it was clearly upsetting customers. I then asked him directly whether, had he previously known the booking was for an LGBT group, he would have refused it. He clearly and unambiguously stated that he would have done and repeated this when I asked the question again.

It wasn't until a few minutes later when one of our members informed me that he had been refused service that we realized this was gong to be a major problem. Bar staff had been told to refuse service to anyone in our group, putting many of the staff in a seriously awkward position. Other patrons of the pub were being served during this time but all of our members were refused.

At about this time the police were called by both one of our members and the member of staff in question. Refusal of service continued until the police arrived. Myself and three other LGBT Labour members then went to the police station to give statements about the discrimination.

Q *Why did you put this on the internet?*

A We wanted other people to know about what was going on so we put it on the website Twitter from the LGBT Labour account almost as soon as we realized that we were being refused service. Our first tweet simply said: 'Appalling homophobia at central London pub. Manager refusing to serve members of #LGBTLabour.'

Q *How quickly did it spread?*

A A number of colleagues and I were distracted from what was happening on Twitter and online due to the arrival of the police. It wasn't until I was in a police car on my way to give a statement that I managed to check the internet on my phone and realized how quickly the news had spread. I was getting fairly constant updates of people informing me that the incident had started trending on Twitter, which means it was one of the most popular topics on the site that afternoon. Then senior political people such as Sarah Brown, the wife of former Prime Minister Gordon Brown, and John Prescott, former Deputy Prime Minister, got involved, and the coverage continued to grow.

Q *Did the traditional media pick up on it?*

A It wasn't long until various media organizations began to show interest in the story and it progressed from there. BBC London News and BBC Radio London were very quick to pick up on the story and ITN also covered it. The story was then covered in papers including the *Guardian*, the *Independent*, the *Daily Mail*, *Pink News*, and the *Pink Paper*, amongst others. It was also the most viewed story on the BBC News website for the weekend.

Q *Did the company that owned the pub respond?*

A The company was quick to get in touch but their initial response was rather feeble. Its original statement apologized that we felt we had been poorly treated but failed to tackle the issue in any substantive manner. Then followed a number of conversations with its public relations and public affairs teams, and a meeting two days later with two members of the management of the group who owned the pub.

Q *What did you learn from this?*

A I was stunned by the amount of support that was shown and how quickly it spread, and I learned that you can't always control what you start. Independently of anything we were doing, people had set up a Facebook group calling on people to boycott the pub which quickly surpassed a thousand members; someone even set up a fake Twitter account pretending to be the PR team of the company that owned the pub.

Serving your community:
The responsibilities of a school governor

Kate Groucutt is a governor at William Tyndale Primary School in the London Borough of Islington. She volunteered to become a governor because she believes passionately in comprehensive education and the benefits that learning in a diverse environment can bring.

Q *Why did you become a school governor?*

A There were several reasons. Partly it was a way of having some sort of connection with the wider community. Living in London it is hard to feel part of a community, especially if you commute into central London for work, and this seemed like a good way to achieve that, since schools are at the heart of the community. And it has worked – I have bumped into fellow governors locally, and when I've been at school events I've spoken to parents, and then met them again through involvement with other community organizations.

But as well as giving something to the community – and getting something back – I wanted to do something more than simply volunteering with an organization, something where I could use my skills but also gain new skills. Also as I work in public policy (currently for the childcare charity Daycare Trust), it was a way of getting a different perspective and seeing how things work on the front line.

Q *What does being a school governor involve?*

A Essentially it involves reading the papers you are sent, turning up to a meeting and discussing them, asking questions, and making collective decisions. So the skills involved are about scrutinizing, examining, making suggestions. We look at policies and strategies, look at the school results, set targets, and support (and hold to account) the headteacher. We often receive presentations from council officers on a particular area – recent examples include sport and improving attendance. I am lucky that my school is rated 'good' by Ofsted, the school inspectors, and that the headteacher is excellent, but there are still often tricky issues to discuss. We also have some pretty important responsibilities, for example around safeguarding and recruitment. I feel we have a duty to make sure we effectively scrutinize what is happening at the school to keep children safe, but also to make sure they get the best possible education that we can offer them.

Q *How much time does it take up?*

A There is one meeting of the full governing body each term, so three per year; these take place in the evening and typically last about two and a half hours, and we go for a drink afterwards. There is also a briefing each term held by the council for all governors at all schools. Then there are committee meetings; at my school these are usually held at 8am, so I can fit them in before work. I am on the finance and curriculum committees. I also go along to school events like the summer fair and fundraising evenings. We get invited to things during the day like school plays and events, but I can't usually go to these. I actually wish I could spend more time at the school, as it is hard to keep track of what is going on when you don't visit it very often. My work is good and gives me the flexibility, but it is still hard to find the time during the day.

Q *What contribution do you feel you make as a governor?*

A I don't have children of my own, so I only have my own memories of school and my judgement to base my comments and decisions on. Other governors have commented that they welcome my contributions, as I bring a different perspective. I can offer an independent voice, as I'm not at the school every day. This is why the mix of governors from parents, staff, and the community is so important. This might mean that although some decisions are a bit uncomfortable for a particular group (for example, the efforts we have made to improve attendance through a tough approach have upset some parents), having the different perspectives means that we make the right decision for children, and the school as a whole.

30

Stop age discrimination

People over the age of fifty-five make up a fifth of the UK's population, yet prejudice based on age is very common in our society. From older people being refused medical treatment and told to expect poor health at their age to insurance services having an age cut off, age discrimination happens frequently, although we may not always realize it. Then there is the language we use around age, often dismissing people's views because they are old or portraying them as confused or old-fashioned rather than someone to be taken seriously.

Further, there is age discrimination in the workplace. Though now illegal, this still goes on, sometimes through informal networks and indirect discrimination, and sometimes in forced retirement and other direct discrimination. The Saga Group, which specializes in products and services for over fifties, notes cases, such as a man in his sixties whose colleagues in their twenties and thirties don't invite him to socialize with them, or a building contractor with a set retirement age of sixty who wishes to carry on working. People are sometimes turned down for a job because they are considered too old (not a 'recent graduate'), or made to feel uncomfortable by comments about their age.

Because making jokes about age is so common, from 'over the hill' gags on birthday cards to quips about dementia if an older person is forgetful, this kind of discrimination is hard to root out. But we must counter it where we can in order to have a fairer society. Or if you need a more selfish reason than that, we will all, hopefully, be old one day, so counter it to protect yourself.

Take Action

▶ *Know your rights.* Age UK has an online guide to age discrimination and what to do if you feel you have been discriminated against. It also runs a freephone advice line.

▶ *Don't discriminate.* Not only is it illegal, it is morally wrong. If you serve in a shop, work in the health service, or recruit people, make sure you treat everybody well, regardless of their age. If you are an employer, don't ask for a date of birth on application forms and don't assume people will want to retire at a certain age.

▶ *Watch your language.* Don't make comments based on people's age and avoid jokes about age or dementia which might make others feel unwanted or vulnerable.

▶ *Speak out.* If you are an older person, or you know an older person who feels strongly about these issues, find an independent local forum that gives older people a voice on local, regional, and national issues. There are over 620 in the UK. Age UK's website has a list of forums and advice on starting your own if there isn't one in your area.

Where to Get Started

Age UK is a charity formed from the merger of two organizations, Age Concern and Help the Aged. It researches, campaigns, and runs services around issues that affect people in later life.
207–221 Pentonville Road
London N1 9UZ
Tel 0800 169 8787
Helpline 0800 169 6565
www.ageuk.org.uk

Making your case: The power of individual stories

Patricia Hollis, Baroness Hollis of Heigham, is a member of the House of Lords. She led the campaign for better state pension provision for women, which was achieved in 2008. Before then, in order to receive a full state pension, women had to have made thirty-nine years of National Insurance contributions while men had to have made forty-four years worth of contributions – which meant that women often fell short; according to the website This Is Money, only 35 per cent of women achieved a full state pension, compared to 90 per cent of men. The campaign achieved a change in the law that allowed people to buy back up to twelve years of missing contributions to ensure they get a full state pension. In 2010 the law improved further, so that both men and women need just thirty years of contributions to receive a full state pension.

Q *Can you explain why the state pension campaign was launched?*

A The problem was that the state pension is based on National Insurance contributions, which means you build up contributions each year by working for a wage in the labour market. This meant that only a small proportion of women were able to retire on a full pension because women often come in and out of the labour market due to looking after children or older people. Although they worked very hard, they didn't get the National Insurance contribution for those years, and while it was possible to buy back the odd year here and there, or to buy back the last six years, many women had missed years longer ago than that. Pensions were based on a working man's life rather than the complex working lives that women lead.

Q *Who had the power to change this?*

A It was a question of persuading the Treasury and the Department of Work and Pensions, as it was then called, that this made good sense. Not only that it was the decent thing to do – recognizing that women's working lives are different to men's – but that it protected women from poverty in old age and a reliance on means-tested benefits.

Q *How did you build a campaign around the state pension issue?*

A The campaign was based on research and background work. I'd been Pensions Minister in the House of Lords for eight years, so I knew how the systems worked and I was able to build an all-party alliance against my own government. In fact, around thirty Labour peers voted against the government or abstained for the first time in their lives. They did so because it was not a party issue, because the costs were modest, and because the benefits for women were enormous.

Helped by the media attention, I must have had a couple of hundred women write to me with their stories. One was a woman called Pam, who had been a dressmaker and then got married and had three children, one of whom was disabled. Her husband left her and she tried to cope by becoming a foster carer. She fostered eighty children over twenty years. When she came to retire she found she only had half a pension because none of that work had given her National Insurance cover. There was another woman who had worked when she was younger, had children, then went back to work. But then her mother and her husband's father became ill, so she became a full-time carer, meaning neither needed residential care – but she got no National Insurance cover for doing this. Then there was the wife of a soldier who had been posted to Cyprus and then Malta, and because she accompanied her husband she couldn't get a job. When they came back she was unable to get her full state pension.

Q *What can people learn from how you organized this campaign?*

A First, you need people to tell you their personal stories and how the situation affects them, and to allow you to use their stories, anonymously if necessary. Second, you need cross-party support for your proposals, which means you have to go for a consensual tone and do it in bite-sized chunks. And third, you have to know your subject and have done your research so when people challenge you the answers are there.

Q *So it's okay to contact members of the House of Lords if you have a campaign you need help with?*

A The public should remember that they can contact members of the House of Lords about their campaigns. In fact, in the House of Lords no party has an overall majority, so it means the government can't win simply by making everyone vote the way it wants – it has to win the argument. But the public have to do their homework and find out which peer is interested in the subject they are concerned about.

31

Let children be children

So much comes under the banner of 'let children be children' – letting children have a carefree, happy childhood whilst also warning them about the dangers some people pose; not sexualizing children through inappropriate behaviour and clothing whilst at the same time acknowledging that children are discovering the sexual side of their nature at their own speed; letting our children take risks and be adventurous and not creating what has been called a 'cotton-wool' childhood whilst at the same time keeping them safe from unnecessary risks. Then there is also the wellbeing of children who are forced to grow up prematurely because they are carers for their parents or must handle other family situations; they too need support – so that they can experience childhood.

It's a fine line between helping children to grow up at their own speed and not putting pressure on them to leave childhood too early, but it's one that we should be dedicated to keeping. Once they enter adulthood, children will never again get the chance to enjoy life without the responsibilities of adulthood.

Take Action

▶ *Vote with your wallet.* If you consider a product aimed at children to be too 'adult', including the use of inappropriate sexy slogans, don't buy it. And write to let the retailer know your concerns.

▶ *Look out for all children.* Watch out for children you see out and about and ensure they are not in danger. If all of society takes on the responsibility of looking out for our children, then parents may feel able to encourage their children to explore and to take 'safe' risks.

▶ *Treat children as children, not mini adults.* Don't sexualize children's relationships or wardrobes, or let them grow up too fast. It's not helpful to label toddlers who are friends as girlfriend and boyfriend, or to let young children wear make-up and high heels outside the dressing up box.

Where to Get Started

Fair Play for Children promotes children's right to play, advises on how play can be organized safely, and lobbies on play-related issues.
32 Longford Road
Bognor Regis PO21 1AG
Tel 0845 330 7635
www.fairplayforchildren.org

The **Children's Society** has a special website providing help and advice for children put into a carer role ('young carers') and their families.
www.youngcarer.com

The **Mumsnet** website has campaigned to stop the premature sexualization of girls through its Let Girls Be Girls campaign. Its talkboards contain lots of advice on this subject.
www.mumsnet.com

The **NSPCC** (the National Society for the Prevention of Cruelty to Children), **Barnardo's**, and many other charities also campaign and run services for the protection of children and for young carers.
Helpline 0808 800 5000
Childline (for children and young people) 0800 1111
NSPCC
Weston House
42 Curtain Road
London EC2A 3NH
Tel 020 7825 2505
www.nspcc.org.uk
Barnardo's
Tanners Lane
Barkingside
Ilford
Essex IG6 1QG
Tel 0208 550 8822
www.barnardos.org.uk

One step at a time:
Combining ambitious ideas with achievable goals

Megan Pacey is Chief Executive at Early Education (www.early-education.org.uk), a charity campaigning for the right of all children to have access to early childhood education of the highest quality. For Pacey, it is ideas rather than money that make a campaign a success.

Q *How ambitious can you be with your campaigns?*

A It's important for campaigns to be progressive and for their process to be one of small-step changes. Lots of small successes add up to significant positive change – even if the campaign objective isn't fully achieved. Many campaigns fail because the process hasn't acknowledged the time needed to win hearts and minds and change attitudes. Rarely are campaigns an overnight success – they are usually the result of decades of work and many hurdles along the way.

Q *What's your top piece of advice for campaigners?*

A Campaign tools for the most part can be really simple. I've never worked for organizations which have had massive campaign budgets, yet some of what I and those organizations have managed to achieve has been highly significant. Having the media – national, local, and trade and both print and broadcast – as your 'campaign mouthpiece' is a must, and taking the time to build relationships with sympathetic journalists who are interested and want to be informed is worth its weight in gold.

Q *Any quirky campaign suggestions?*

A One of the techniques we used when I was involved with a childcare campaign was to write to the scriptwriters at the soap operas *EastEnders* and *Coronation Street* and request that they include stories about the challenges of childcare. We sent them a selection of our briefing material that detailed some of the sorts of parents who really struggled with childcare – students, shift workers, parents with children with a disability, teenage parents, and so on. Before we knew it, we were seeing storylines that reflected some of these issues, such as a character in *Coronation Street* who was a teenage parent and was involved in a campaign to save the nursery that her daughter went to at her college so that she could continue her studies. We were particularly elated when we spotted a National Childcare Month poster on the noticeboard in the Cafe in *EastEnders*.

32

Say no to child labour

The use of child labour is one of the most chilling ways in which children are forced out of childhood long before they should be. According to Unicef (the United Nations Children's Fund), there are an estimated 158 million children aged five to fourteen who are engaged in child labour – one in six children in the world. Many millions of these work in dangerous conditions, including working in mines, working with chemicals, and working with machinery. Others are employed in domestic labour or workshops, often producing consumer goods for people in developed countries.

In some countries, children are even conscripted into armies, where they face down fellow child soldiers who have met a similar fate on the other side of a war. Children involved in armed conflict are frequently killed or injured during combat or while carrying out other tasks. They are forced to engage in hazardous activities, such as laying mines or explosives, as well as using weapons. Child soldiers are usually forced to live under harsh conditions with insufficient food and little or no access to healthcare. They are almost always treated brutally, subjected to beatings and humiliating treatment. Punishments for mistakes or desertion are often very severe. Girl soldiers are particularly at risk of sexual harassment, sexual abuse, and rape as well as being involved in combat and other tasks. According to the social justice internet portal OneWorld Network, 250,000 children serve in the armies of fourteen countries, including Sudan, Nepal, Iran, and Colombia.

Child labour, in the workplace or in the military, not only robs children of what we consider to be a normal childhood, with the chance to play and develop at their own pace, but also usually prevents them from going to school and getting an education that might enable them to ensure their own children are not forced to work, too.

Take Action

▶ *Protest with your wallet.* Try not to buy products that you think have been produced by child labour. It is hard to determine this, so look for shops that have publicly stated ethics policies. For example, one of the aims of the Fairtrade Foundation (see page 64) is ensuring that no child labour is involved in the manufacture of the goods with its seal.

▶ *Forge links across the world.* Try to foster links between children in your community and children forced to work living in other countries, by suggesting child labour as a topic of discussion for a school or youth group you are involved with. Oxfam can provide assembly plans for schools on this and other issues.

▶ *Get the decision makers on your side.* If the government in the country in which you live has not already done so, urge it to sign and ratify the Optional Protocol to the Convention on the Rights of the Child on the involvement of children in armed conflict, which specifies a minimum age of eighteen for all forms of military recruitment; to ratify the Statute of the International Criminal Court, which addresses the recruitment and use of children under fifteen; and to adopt at the very least the International Labour Organization Conventions 182 and 190 on the Worst Forms of Child Labour. You can also contact your elected representatives asking what they are doing to stop the involvement of under-eighteens in armed conflict at home and abroad.

Where to Get Started

Many charities work towards ending child labour. These include **Concern Worldwide** (www.concern.net), **Oxfam** (www.oxfam.org.uk), **Unicef** (www.unicef.org), and **War on Want** (www.waronwant.org).

The **Stop Child Labour** campaign seeks to eliminate child labour through the provision of full-time formal education.
PO Box 85565
2508 CG The Hague
The Netherlands
Tel +31 (0)70 376 5500
www.stopchildlabour.eu

The **Coalition to Stop the Use of Child Soldiers** wants to prevent the recruitment of child soldiers, secure their demobilization, and promote their rehabilitation and reintegration into society by working with networks in Africa, Asia, Europe, Latin America, and the Middle East. The coalition's member organizations are Amnesty International, Human Rights Watch, International Federation Terre des Hommes, International Save the Children Alliance, and the Jesuit Refugee Service. It maintains active links with Unicef, the International Committee of the Red Cross, and the International Labour Organization.
4th Floor, 9 Marshalsea Road
London SE1 1EP
Tel 020 7367 4110
www.child-soldiers.org

The human cost:
The blood diamonds campaign

Paul Eagle is Business and Human Rights Adviser at Amnesty International UK (www.amnesty.org.uk). One of his campaigns worked to raise awareness of 'blood diamonds', or 'conflict diamonds', which are diamonds mined, sometimes using slave or conscripted labour, to fund an army's or insurgency's war efforts. Blood diamonds are believed to have been used to support conflicts in Angola, Liberia, Sierra Leone, and elsewhere. The campaign focused on using consumer power and the publicity around a Hollywood film to help highlight the issue.

Q *Can you explain what the campaign was and who your partners were?*

A Amnesty worked in partnership with the group Global Witness (www.globalwitness.org) on the conflict diamonds campaign. We used research from Global Witness combined with our network of activists as a joint force to highlight the issues around these diamonds, including the concern that the Kimberley Process, a UN process in which governments, industry, and civil society work together to stem the flow of conflict diamonds, needed strengthening.

Q *How did you make use of your activists?*

A Our activists, mainly in the UK, the USA, and mainland Europe, were asked over a period of weeks to go into diamond shops and jewellery stores, both chains and independents, and ask five or six simple questions about their diamonds. These ranged from whether they had heard of the term 'blood diamonds' or 'conflict diamonds' to whether they had training in the Kimberley certification process. Amnesty then mapped the responses they got and Global Witness produced a report on the survey. We wanted to highlight the discrepancy between what the companies said their policies were at a head office level and how they were being implemented in the shops. We also produced what looked like a marketing leaflet for diamonds but inside it laid out the issue in simple terms and listed the questions people should ask before buying a diamond.

Q *What impact did this have?*

A We had some success – some of the companies realized there were lots of potential customers asking questions, which received extensive media coverage. These companies became worried that their image might be tarnished because people might think they were selling conflict diamonds if they didn't know the answers to the questions, so they changed their policies and improved the training of their staff.

Q *Was the Hollywood film about the subject a help to the campaign?*

A This was all happening in 2006, around the time the film *Blood Diamond*, starring Leonardo DiCaprio, was released, so we also had an arrangement with the film's producers and distributors that, providing we negotiated directly with local cinemas, we could set up a stall about the issue in the foyer when the film was being shown. We also had local Amnesty International showings in cities around the UK. In addition, Global Witness, who had worked with the film's director, and Amnesty International UK held a premiere of the film for a selected audience in London.

33

Stop human trafficking

Humans are not commodities to be bought and sold like you might a sack of grain, a plastic toy, or a share in a company. But today there are more people bought and sold against their will than there were during the legal slave trade. It's estimated that up to 800,000 people are trafficked across international borders every year. They are forced to work in the sex industry, domestic service, or other areas. Some are even forced to donate organs. The majority of these people are women, and most cases of human trafficking include a level of sexual exploitation.

Take for example the story of a twenty-four-year-old Eastern European woman Maria, whose story is told on the UK's Serious Organised Crime Agency's (SOCA) website. Sold by her abusive family to a stranger, she was taken to Italy, sold again, and raped. Police were alerted by neighbours, and Maria was taken to a nunnery for shelter. Two years later she returned to her family, only to be sold and taken to Italy again. This time, she was transported on to the UK. Here she was forced for five years to work as a prostitute, seeing between sixty-five and eighty customers a day.

Another case highlighted by SOCA is of a twenty-eight-year-old woman who, unemployed and desperate for a job, answered an advert in the paper to be an au pair in London. She paid money for a visa and for her trip, and came to London believing she was travelling legally, only to be told by her traffickers when she arrived that she owed them £320,000 and would have to work as a prostitute to pay them back.

This modern slavery is a problem throughout the world. According to the United Nations, victims of trafficking have been taken from 127 countries and exploited in 137 countries – which means there are almost certainly people in your community or nearby who have been brought there against their will, through trickery, lies, or kidnapping. It is the responsibility of all of us to notice their plight and to do something about it.

Take Action

▶ *Notice the signs of captivity.* A percentage of sex workers are held against their will. If you do visit a sex worker, whether a lap dancer or a prostitute, ask the person if he or she is there willingly. Does he or she only know sex-related words in English? Does he or she appear frightened? These are signs that he or she is there against his or her will, and these signs should not be ignored.

▶ *Keep an eye on local businesses.* In addition to sex work, some industries are known for using forced labour; flower picking is one. Ask your flower shop or supermarket if it can guarantee its flowers come from farms that do not use trafficked or exploited labour. You can also scan the newspapers for stories about businesses being raided for using forced labour to get a sense of the industries that may be trouble spots.

▶ *Report the crime.* Contact the police about any concerns about trafficking you have. You can do this anonymously in the UK by calling the Crimestoppers helpline on 0800 555 111.

Where to Get Started

Blue Blindfold encourages awareness of human trafficking among police authorities, health professionals, and the general public. It also supports victims of trafficking.
PO Box 4107
Sheffield S1 9DQ
Tel 0114 252 3891
www.blueblindfold.co.uk

Amnesty International fights human trafficking, as well as other injustices and human rights abuses around the world.

Human Rights Action Centre
17–25 New Inn Yard
London EC2A 3EA
Tel 020 7033 1500
www.amnesty.org.uk

Stop the Traffik is a coalition of over 900 member organizations from over fifty countries, working together to fight against human trafficking.
75 Westminster Bridge Road
London SE1 7HS
Tel 020 7291 4258
www.stopthetraffik.org

The definition of human trafficking

THE RECRUITMENT, TRANSPORTATION, transfer, harbouring, or receipt of persons, by means of the threat or use of force or other forms of coercion, of abduction, of fraud, of deception, of the abuse of power, or of a position of vulnerability or of the giving or receiving of payments or benefits to achieve the consent of a person having control over another person, for the purpose of exploitation.

Source: The United Nations.

34

Control the arms trade

It is estimated that one thousand people die each day from armed violence and 26 million people are currently displaced within their own countries by armed conflict. Yet, there are no legally binding international rules governing the arms trade, and national controls are exploited to ensure arms get to conflict zones and human rights abusers.

There is a global campaign to stop the unregulated international arms trade. Spearheaded by Amnesty International, the International Action Network on Small Arms, and Oxfam, the Control Arms campaign has lobbied hard for measures that will control the flow of weapons around the world, including presenting a 'Million Faces' petition to UN Secretary General Kofi Annan in 2006, the year the UN General Assembly began work towards writing an historic arms trade treaty. Today, the campaign's emphasis is on ensuring the UN's treaty is strongly worded to prevent the sale of arms that are likely to fuel conflict or poverty or be used for serious human rights violations.

Of course, not all arms are gained through the international market; many weapons and munitions are produced locally. But a large proportion is sourced through the international arms trade, and while there are legitimate arms deals such as those for self defence, peacekeeping, and law enforcement, we need to ensure that arms do not end up in the hands of groups that commit human rights abuses and war crimes.

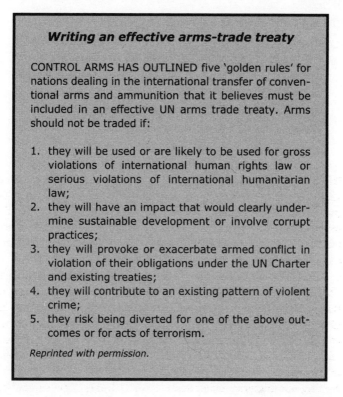

Writing an effective arms-trade treaty

CONTROL ARMS HAS OUTLINED five 'golden rules' for nations dealing in the international transfer of conventional arms and ammunition that it believes must be included in an effective UN arms trade treaty. Arms should not be traded if:

1. they will be used or are likely to be used for gross violations of international human rights law or serious violations of international humanitarian law;
2. they will have an impact that would clearly undermine sustainable development or involve corrupt practices;
3. they will provoke or exacerbate armed conflict in violation of their obligations under the UN Charter and existing treaties;
4. they will contribute to an existing pattern of violent crime;
5. they risk being diverted for one of the above outcomes or for acts of terrorism.

Reprinted with permission.

Take Action

▶ *Sign up.* Join the Million Faces petition on the Control Arms website.

▶ *Ask your representatives to sign up, too.* Write to your MP to ask him or her to sign the Parliamentarians' Declaration, which calls on all governments to move quickly towards the negotiation of a tough arms trade treaty.

Where to Get Started

Control Arms campaigns for a global,
legally binding arms trade treaty.
1 Easton Street
London WC1X 0DW
Tel 020 7413 5500
www.controlarms.org

35

Protect indigenous peoples

It is thought that 370 million individuals worldwide identify as indigenous or tribal peoples. Unfortunately, around the world the homes, cultures, and livelihoods of these peoples are being threatened, and their human rights are being ignored.

Tribal peoples are in some instances subject to systematic massacres, genocides, armed conflicts, development, discriminatory government policies, or private economic interests, and sometimes by a combination of these forces. Take the peoples of the Omo Valley area in southwest Ethiopia. There, 200,000 people live in eight tribes whose future is threatened by the construction of a hydroelectric dam that will wipe out the seasonal flood plain on which they cultivate food. Or consider the Penan people in Sarawak, on the island of Borneo, who have no recognized land rights from the state of Malaysia, and whose hunter-gatherer lifestyle is threatened by the clearing of forests for logging. Without the necessary resources, and away from the community structures and traditions they are used to, these tribal peoples may face marginalization, poverty, disease, and violence – possibly, as Amnesty International warns, even extinction as a people.

Many organizations are working to support indigenous and tribal peoples by raising awareness of what is happening to them, so that the weight of public opinion can put pressure on governments and companies to stop practices that could see the end of whole cultures, languages, and ways of life. And others are working to save the environments in which tribal people live, including rainforests. According to the Rainforest Foundation, each year an area of rainforest the size of England and Wales is cut down – a great loss of resources to the people who live there.

The United Nations Declaration on the Rights of Indigenous Peoples was adopted in September 2007. It reaffirms the right of indigenous and tribal peoples to have meaningful control over their own lives, to maintain their distinct cultural identities, to live free from discrimination and the threat of genocide, and to have secure access to the lands and resources essential to their wellbeing and ways of life. It is vital that we continue to put pressure on politicians around the world to stick to these standards.

Take Action

▶ *Challenge the government.* Survival International urges people to write letters to the government in countries in which tribal peoples are under threat. Letters have been sent to the prime minister of Australia about the health problems of Aboriginal people and to the president of Peru about violence against the indigenous communities of the Amazon. SI's website provides letter templates that you can use.

▶ *Educate others.* Host a film night about the culture and struggles of tribal peoples (DVDs are also available from SI) or ask for some literature to display at your work, school, or local library.

Where to Get Started

Survival International supports tribal peoples worldwide through education, advocacy, and campaigns.
6 Charterhouse Buildings
London EC1M 7ET
Tel 020 7687 8700
www.survivalinternational.org

The **Rainforest Foundation** supports indigenous peoples and traditional populations of the world's rainforest, including trying to secure and control the natural resources necessary for their long-term wellbeing and developing the means to protect their individual and collective rights.
2nd Floor, Imperial Works
Perren Street
London NW5 3ED
Tel 020 7485 0193
www.rainforestfoundationuk.org

Putting your money where your mouth is:
Top tips for fundraising

Having money can give a campaign access to essential resources; not having it can stall your efforts. Four professional fundraisers offer their advice for raising money effectively.

From Kirstie Hayward, Individual Giving Fundraiser at the Rainforest Foundation UK (www.rainforestfoundationuk.org):

- Make it personal. People like to give to people. A case study with one person or family always seems to attract more support than talking about the hundreds of thousands of people affected.
- You don't always need to spend a fortune to make a fortune. A personal letter with a photo attached can be far more effective than a huge glossy appeal pack, especially if you can make it as personal as possible.
- Get to know your donors. The best way to build a lasting relationship with a donor is to get to know them. For a larger donation or interesting fundraising story pick up the phone. You'll probably remember them and they'll probably remember you.
- Save paper. I am a big fan of thanking donors no matter how small the donation. However, many would rather you saved the paper and the postage. A personal email from your own email address (rather than, say, support@ ...) can be just as personal – plus, you often get a response, which helps build that relationship further.

- Stand out. A person who gives to charity is more likely to give to another charity than a person who has never given. This means a large percentage of your database will be receiving numerous requests for support. So make sure your ideas stand out from the crowd.

From Kristen Lindop, Fundraiser at Young People's Trust for the Environment (www.ypte.org.uk):

- Say thank you, and keep saying it. Funders are not obliged to give, no matter how important we consider our cause, and we owe a debt of gratitude to all those who support our work.
- Accentuate the positive. The problems you want to address are important, but it's the solutions you provide that will inspire the funder to give.
- Communication is key. Regular updates are important, but so are phone calls, visits, and invitations to events and to view work in progress.

From Annu Mayor, Director of Fundraising at Fight for Sight (www.fightforsight.org.uk):

- Plan your activity. Think about the activities you enjoy and how much time and help you have available. There are lots of ways you can fundraise, from hosting an event to holding a collection to organizing a sponsored activity.
- Keep it legal. Check with the charity if you need any special permissions or licenses for your fundraising. For example, if you are holding public collections or raffles, or are planning to sell alcohol, you may need a licence from your local authority.
- Encourage support. If you are collecting sponsorships, kick off by asking a generous donor to make the first pledge. This will encourage others to be as generous!
- Make donations go further. Make sure you ask your supporters to Gift Aid their donations (if they're

eligible). The Gift Aid scheme allows charities to reclaim the tax on donations made. [See page 182 for more on Gift Aid.]

- Use the internet. Set up a Just Giving page (www.just-giving.com). It is easy to collect donations online and you can include a link at the bottom of your emails, on your Facebook page, and on other internet profiles.
- Don't be afraid to ask. Ask your employer if they will match the amount you raise. Companies often support their employees' fundraising in this way.
- Get noticed. Ask the charity if they can provide T-shirts, balloons, and other materials for events and collections. It will help to get you and the charity's name noticed.

From Lucy Lloyd-Ruck, Fundraising Officer at Disability Sport Events (www.disabilitysport.org.uk):

- Enjoy it. Fundraising is fun. Choose a cause that you're passionate about and an event that you'll enjoy organizing to maximize your fundraising experience.
- Know your costs. Know how much you want to fundraise and how you're going to achieve it and keep the event costs down. The lower the costs, the less risk to your fundraising event. This will allow you to work out, for instance, how many tickets you need to sell to meet your fundraising target.
- Plan ahead. The most successful fundraising events are those that are planned in detail. Make sure your event is timely and does not coincide with others. Give yourself plenty of time to organize.
- Market your event. Promote your event to family, friends, work colleagues, or the general public. Make sure that you use tools such as Facebook, Twitter, posters, and leaflets. The more people you tell, the more will attend your event. Create a buzz: contact your local newspaper, radio, or TV station.

36

End hunger

According to Oxfam, a child dies every five seconds due to a hunger related cause. Sometimes this hunger is the direct result of something unusual happening – a war or a natural disaster. Sometimes it's part of the constant struggle to make enough money to buy food.

Around 967 million people in the world at the moment are hungry. The number is practically incomprehensible. But as individuals they are not – they are, as Oxfam says, children, brothers, sisters, neighbours, and friends. The lack of food facing the world's poor leads to almost unimaginable decisions – choosing which child to feed, or whether to buy food or medicine. This has been made worse by the worldwide recession, which has led to high food prices and less trade. Hunger is not just a problem in developing countries. According to the End Hunger Network there are 16.7 million American children – nearly one in four – living in households that do not have access to enough nutritious food to lead healthy, active lives.

It's one of the great travesties of our age, and hard to believe that in a world where there is so much, so many people don't get enough food to keep them alive.

Take Action

▶ *Raise awareness and funds.* The main way you can help end hunger involves increasing support for the appropriate agencies in the developing world which work on the ground. These agencies have the infrastructure and expertise to ensure that aid and food supplies go to the needy.

Where to Get Started

Action Against Hunger (also known as ACF International) is a global humanitarian organization committed to ending world hunger and malnutrition. It works to provide food to malnourished children and provide communities with access to safe water and long-term, sustainable solutions to hunger.
First Floor, Rear Premises
161–163 Greenwich High Road
London SE10 8JA
Tel 020 8293 6190
www.actionagainsthunger.org

Oxfam seeks to overcome poverty and hunger around the world.
Oxfam House
John Smith Drive
Cowley
Oxford OX4 2JY
Tel 0300 200 1300
www.oxfam.org.uk

In the beginning:
The importance of the idea

Adrian Lovett was Deputy Director of the Jubilee 2000 campaign to drop the debt. He is now Campaigns Director at Save the Children (www.savethechildren.org.uk).

Q *Tell us about Jubilee 2000.*

A Before anyone ever wrote a strategy or started building a brand, there was an idea. Jubilee 2000 and the Drop the Debt campaign began with a brilliant idea as the best campaigns do. The idea was that we could make the millennium moment meaningful by doing something extraordinary – cancelling the debt of the poorest countries as a one-off for the millennium.

In the UK in the late 1990s, there were lots of questions about what the millennium was meant to be. The main marker was the Millennium Dome being built in London, and that just didn't seem to measure up. So the Jubilee 2000 idea caught on, partly because it was a great idea and partly because there was a hunger to fill that gap in meaning.

The idea first came about in the late 1980s and early 1990s from two people, Bill Peters, a former diplomat, and Martin Dent, a retired academic. At the same time there was a more conventional campaign around debt called the Debt Crisis Network, which was a coalition of charities and NGOs. They were doing policy focused work, putting across the idea that debt in the developing world was unsustainable and that it stopped developing countries from investing in schools and health and so on. In the mid-1990s these two worlds came together – the unconventional and hard-to-pin-down energy with a lot of moral force came together with a more institutional, policy-based lobbying focus. They combined to become the Jubilee 2000 coalition.

Q *How did it go from being an idea to becoming a campaign?*

A This wonderfully powerful idea was backed by an organizational base – we had about 150 organizations join us, from the Socialist Workers Party to the Scouts. It was that diversity that was part of the power of the coalition, because you can have the best idea in the world, but it's nothing without a network to put the idea out there.

By 1999 there were Jubilee 2000 campaigns in about sixty countries, including in the indebted countries themselves, where the campaigners wanted to make sure the money from debt cancellation went where it was needed. We also had a very strong-minded and forceful director, Ann Pettifor. She was able to stand up in meetings of the World Bank in Washington, DC, or the Treasury in London and say, 'this isn't just an issue for economists but something people around the world care about'. That was very unusual for people to hear in those days.

Q *What did you ask supporters to do?*

A We asked supporters to write handwritten letters to Treasury officials. These couldn't have been further from the orthodox, policy-based papers these officials were used to reading – one official remarked how a letter he received was on flowery paper and written in lilac ink. And as the campaign reached its peak, Gordon Brown, then chancellor of the exchequer, even spoke about how he received one of the campaign postcards from his mum.

We also decided that the G8 summit was something worth focusing on. Back in 1998, when the G8 met in Birmingham, England, it was quite an unusual thing for them to face interest, let alone any challenges, from people in the host country. Through our various networks we put together 70,000 people to form a human chain around Birmingham. We said to people that if they did one thing that year could it please be to be there in Birmingham that day. And at the last minute Prime Minister Tony Blair asked to meet with the campaign leaders. We didn't really get any results out of that G8, but we did the next year, when the G8 was in Cologne, Germany. What we did in Birmingham made that possible.

Q *Why do you think the campaign worked?*

A Part of the campaign's success was down to having a government that was willing to listen and to play its part. That was the case in a number of countries. US President Bill Clinton said of Jubilee 2000, 'I know a big tent when I see one'; he was impressed by the range of organizations supporting us, from evangelical churches to left-wing trade unionists.

A lot of what we did doesn't feel that imaginative. For example, we had a petition. But we decided not just to have a petition but to have the world's largest petition. We discovered that meant getting over 20 million signatures and we got around 24 million signatures in the end. We had things like the Millennium Write Down Book, where we asked people to write down their hopes for the new millennium in huge books that we took to town halls and churches and community centres. We took these books to Downing Street to present to the prime minister at the end of that year. Our symbol was also good. We had the 2000 written in numbers with the zeroes looking like a chain. The idea was we wanted to break the chains of debt but we also wanted to forge a human chain.

Q *Has the campaign finished?*

A We didn't get everything we wanted from the campaign, but we did get about £50 billion debt cancellation, which was about a third of the total debt owed by those countries at the time. We described it as getting halfway up the mountain – no mean feat and it feels like you have come a long way, but it doesn't mean you don't have farther to go. Lots of people felt the campaign should carry on, but we had created it because of a particular moment and we decided it was right to let it change into something else once the moment had passed.

I now work at Save the Children. Over the next few years we have a campaign that very much builds on the spirit of Jubilee 2000 called Every One. It's based on the idea that of the 9 million children's lives that are lost every year, every one of those has the same right to survive and every one of us can do something about it by giving money, time, or our commitment.

37

Avoid wasting food

Remember teachers and lunchtime assistants at school checking your plate and telling you to eat up all your dinner because there were starving children in the world? Perhaps you were – or still are – one of the wise kids who brandished the ultimate retort to their chiding: Well, why don't you just airlift the leftovers to those starving children, then? While this would be a ludicrous approach to alleviating hunger around the world, there is a case to be made for wasting less food in rich countries.

In the UK, 8.3 million tonnes of food is thrown away by households every year according to the Love Food Hate Waste campaign. That's the equivalent of over 200,000 slices of bread. Some of this food is natural wastage of course: bones and vegetable peelings, egg shells and teabags. But much of it is food that is perfectly edible – or was, that is, until it went off.

On the most basic level, this is a waste of money. But the people ditching their leftover potatoes, throwing away their meat carcasses, and tossing aside browning fruit aren't just burning through hard-earned pennies; when food gets bought up and thrown out, there is a massive environmental impact. Every bit of food has a carbon footprint, be it the energy taken to produce the food, to pack it, or to transport it to the shop up the High Street. For example, according to University of Manchester research published by the BBC, a turkey dinner for eight generates twenty kilograms of carbon dioxide emissions, making your Christmas dinner equivalent to 6000 car journeys around the world,. Waste the food and all of this energy is wasted, too.

Take Action

▶ *Learn to cook properly*. Develop a flair for dishes that take advantage of leftovers, such as soups, salads, and stews. Then hold a cooking party where you and your friends share recipes and ideas.

▶ *Plan the menu*. Map out your recipes for the week and don't buy more food than you need. Expect that you might have leftovers some nights. Save them and turn them into dinner for the next day, before they go off.

Make soup

MOST VEGETABLE AND MEAT leftovers can be turned into soup. If you are using leftover raw ingredients, gently fry the veg until they are soft and the meat, if you are using any, until it is cooked. If the leftovers are already cooked just add them to a pot. Add stock, water, or milk in any combination, depending on whether you like a clear soup or creamy soup; the more liquid, the thinner the soup. You can save and refrigerate water from cooking veg for a very basic soup stock, or use the pieces of the veg you'd usually throw away, like broccoli stalks, celery leaves, and peelings, to make your soup more flavourful. Season to taste and add herbs like thyme or parsley near the end to ensure they keep their flavour. You can serve the soup chunky like a stew or use a food processor to make it smooth. Add a can or carton of beans if you want something more substantial. You can toast torn-up pieces of leftover bread to make croutons, too.

▶ *Start a compost heap*. If you can't use up all your food, at least put it to some use. You can also ask your local authority if it has a food waste collection, and if it doesn't, lobby it to start one.

Where to Get Started

Love Food, Hate Waste aims to raise awareness of the need to reduce the amount of food that we throw away, and the benefit to consumers and the environment if less food is wasted. It is funded by the UK government.
The Old Academy
21 Horse Fair
Banbury OX16 0AH
Helpline 0845 600 0323
www.lovefoodhatewaste.com

38

Ensure access to clean water

Water is probably the world's most important resource. Access to clean water and to good sanitation is essential for a person's health and livelihood. For that reason, the United Nations recognizes the right to water as an essential human right.

Yet for many people in the world, particularly in developing nations, access to clean water and safe sanitation is poor. Approximately one in eight of the world's population – 884 million people – do not have access to safe water. In even starker terms, one child dies every twenty seconds from diarrhoea caused by unclean water and poor sanitation. With improved access to clean water, many of these deaths would be preventable.

There are other serious repercussions to poor sanitation, water, and hygiene. According to Unicef, children, particularly girls, are denied their right to education because their schools lack private and decent sanitation facilities; and women have to spend large parts of the day fetching water. What's more, farms are less productive, and that makes sustainable development impossible. Health systems become overwhelmed, too.

Take Action

▶ *Learn more*. The charity WaterAid has a network of over 400 speakers in the UK who can talk about what it means to a community to lack access to safe water. Invite a speaker to your youth group, community group, workplace, or school. You can also volunteer to become a speaker yourself. The charity provides a lot of resources on its website for preparing your talks.

▶ *Refill the well.* Money is essential to providing wells, toilets, and sanitation technology in the world's poorest communities, and every penny helps. Think about refilling your water bottle at home instead of buying bottled water and donating your savings to a charity working in the field.

Where to Get Started

WaterAid seeks to improve access to safe water, hygiene, and sanitation in the world's poorest communities.
47–49 Durham Street
London SE11 5JD
Tel 020 7793 4594
www.wateraid.org

Unicef (the United Nations Children's Fund) works in over ninety countries to improve water supplies and sanitation facilities in schools and communities, and to promote safe hygiene practices.
UK Helpdesk
2 Kingfisher House
Woodbrook Crescent
Billericay CM12 0EQ
Tel 0844 801 2414
www.unicef.org.uk

Down to basics:
Payroll Giving and Gift Aid

Payroll Giving

Payroll Giving is a scheme that allows anyone who pays income tax in the UK to give money to charity on a tax-free basis. Your contribution is taken from your salary before tax is deducted, which effectively means that for each £1.00 the charity receives it will only cost you 80p (60p if you are a higher-rate tax payer). There is no minimum or maximum amount you can give, and the amount you give will be shown on your payslip so you can keep track of your donations.

You can give money in this way to any UK registered charity, even a small local one that is not well known. All you need is their registered charity number.

Payroll Giving has increased substantially in the last ten years, with £106 million given in this way in 2009–2010 compared to £37 million in 1999–2000. But currently only 4 per cent of employers participate in the Payroll Giving scheme in the UK (compared to 35 per cent in the USA). It is estimated that if participation in the UK could grow to 10 per cent, charities would receive an extra £300 million annually.

Information about joining the scheme, or asking your employer to join the scheme, can be found at the Payroll Giving website, www.payrollgiving.co.uk.

Gift Aid

Gift Aid is a scheme administered by HM Revenue & Customs that allows charities and community amateur sports clubs (CASC) to increase the value of donations by 'reclaiming' tax on your gift. The scheme is for gifts of money by individuals who are UK taxpayers, and as such the donation is assumed to come from money on which you have already paid tax, such as your salary, savings interest (where tax is deducted at source), state pension and other pensions, investment or rental income, or capital gains.

In order to allow a charity or CASC to claim Gift Aid, you'll need to fill out a Gift Aid declaration, which is usually a simple form provided by the charity in which you give your name, home address, the name of the charity, and the details of your donation. If you are donating money, then do ask about making this declaration at the time of your donation.

Information about Gift Aid can be found at HM Revenue & Customs website, www.hmrc.gov.uk.

39

Recycle everything

So much of what we use in our day-to-day lives can be recycled, but because we don't know this, or it isn't always made easy for us, just a small percentage of what can be recycled actually is. It's embarrassing to realize that UK households dump more waste into landfill than those in any other country in Europe.

Reusing and recycling makes sense for many reasons. If we recycle, then we reduce the need for new products, thus decreasing the demand for resources to be got through mining or forestry, thus conserving these materials as well as protecting the natural environment. Recycling also saves energy, as it takes less energy to recycle something than to produce a new product from raw materials. Plus, less landfill means less methane, a greenhouse gas that contributes towards climate warming.

Take Action

▶ *Give things away*. Freecycle (www.uk.freecycle.org) is a local **network** where people put things they no longer need on offer for **others** to pick up for free, preventing things from going to landfill.

▶ *Educate yourself*. Find out what you can recycle or reuse – it is often more than you think. For example, opticians collect old glasses for charities, recycling centres often collect leftover paint for reuse, and even old keys can be recycled with general scrap metal.

Where to Get Started

Recycle Now has an online guide to
what can be recycled in the UK.
www.recyclenow.com

40

Use reusable bags

Environmentally unfriendly and viewed by many as disposable, plastic bags are perhaps the most obvious sign of our throwaway culture. Recently we have seen a backlash against the plastic bag: some countries have introduced a bag tax, and many companies now charge for plastic bags; some towns, such as Modbury in Devon, have banned them altogether. Even the fashion industry embraced the anti-plastic bag bandwagon, spawning the famous Anya Hindmarch cloth bag that proclaimed 'I'm not a plastic bag'.

Although there is an environmental cost in producing plastic bags, banning them is not necessarily the answer. Scientists see the environmental cost of producing plastic bags as a small problem when considering the larger picture of climate change. Plus, banning or taxing plastic bags can have unintended consequences, including a higher demand for alternative products such as bin liners.

But their use does cause huge problems, perhaps the biggest of which is the damage they cause when throwing them away. The *Guardian* reported that in South Africa plastic bags became known ironically as the 'new national flower', so many of them littered the roadsides before a ban on super-lightweight bags was introduced in 2008. And marine animals can mistake plastic bags in the water for jelly fish and swallow them or become tangled up in them, with tens of thousands of whales, birds, seals, and turtles dying as a result every year.

Take Action

▶ *Pack your bags*. Very simply, always carry a reusable non-plastic bag with you and ask others you know to do the same.

Where to Get Started

Friends of the Earth campaigns on
environmental issues including packaging,
recycling, and the use of plastic bags.
26–28 Underwood Street
London N1 7JQ
Tel 020 7490 1555
www.foe.co.uk

Getting attention every time

'I WORK IN PUBLIC relations specializing in small charities. Promotions, stunts, and a bit of local knowledge can make a real difference to campaigns – especially when you are on a tight budget.

For example, when the Bulwell Community Toy Library in Nottingham, England, wanted to raise awareness of their services to families, they went one better than handing out flyers. They sold key rings branded with their logo for £1.00, which were designed to fit into supermarket trolleys in place of the usual £1 coin. The result? The toy library got their message about helping families across, not just once but every time people used their key rings, plus busy parents didn't have to worry about finding a £1 coin whenever they went shopping. By selling the key rings, the charity covered the cost of the campaign and raised money on top.

Another Nottingham charity, the Partnership Council, didn't spend a penny on its recycling campaign. It simply made costumes out of 'rubbish' which staff and volunteers wore to grab people's attention outside a local supermarket. It timed the campaign to coincide with the day the supermarket opened its new recycling facilities. The unusual and amusing costumes got shoppers talking whilst the charity gave away recycled carrier bags and information on how to recycle.'

Stephanie Robertson, PR consultant, 13 Souls

41

Push for more and safer cycling

There is an efficient, cheap, healthy, and green solution to getting around that involves neither the use of public transport nor walking: cycling. During an urban rush hour, cycling is much faster than taking a car. Bikes require no road tax, no MOT, no insurance, no licensing, no breakdown recovery services, and no fuel. What's more, according to the British Heart Foundation, cycling at least twenty miles a week reduces the risk of heart disease to less than half that for non-cyclists. It is, cyclists maintain, an excellent environmentally friendly way to get from point A to B.

Yet despite its benefits, cycling is not made very easy in the UK. We lack the services and support found in several other European countries, where cycle lanes are the norm and not to own a bike is seen as unusual, whatever your age.

We need more cycle lanes and for roads to be properly maintained, as potholes are a real danger for cyclists. We need safer places to lock up our bikes, to encourage more people to buy them, and for other road users to have a better awareness of cyclists so that there are fewer accidents. We also need more safety training, perhaps as part of compulsory cycling proficiency exams. And of course, we need cyclists to take responsibility for making the roads safer too – by stopping at red lights, not using the pavement, and generally cycling responsibly.

Take Action

▶ *Become a cycle ranger.* Volunteer rangers are appointed by the charity Sustrans to monitor a specific section of the National Cycle Network near their home. They deal with minor problems. for example cutting back overgrown vegetation, and report major problems such as missing signs, potholes, and other hazards.

▶ *Help schools become cycle friendly.* Support walking and cycling projects that help children get to local schools, by helping ensure the route is safe. If your school doesn't have a cycling scheme, suggest it starts one. And ask your school or workplace to ensure there are adequate and safe places to lock up bikes.

▶ *Get a tax incentive.* Ask your employer to introduce a tax-free bike scheme to help employees to purchase a bike to use to get to work.

> *When I see an adult on a bicycle, I do not despair for the*
> *future of the human race*
> HG WELLS

Where to Get Started

Sustrans is the UK's leading sustainable transport charity. It lobbies for policies that allow more people to travel in ways that benefit their health and the environment.
2 Cathedral Square
College Green
Bristol BS1 5DD
Tel 0117 926 8893
www.sustrans.org.uk

CTC is the UK's national cyclists' organization and works to protect and promote the rights of cyclists.
Parklands
Railton Road
Guildford
Surrey GU2 9JX
Tel 0844 736 8450
www.ctc.org.uk

Whycycle is an online forum offering impartial advice for potential cyclists in the UK.
www.whycycle.co.uk

42

Clean up our beaches and protect our seas

Water makes up nearly 70 per cent of the earth's surface. It is essential to maintaining the earth's climate and it is home to important and diverse ecosystems. Yet we use the seas as the world's dustbin. We can see this from the waste that washes up on our beaches, and from the 'plastic soup' of rubbish that has accumulated in some ocean regions, covering an area twice the size of the USA in the Pacific Ocean alone. Indeed, a recent study by the United Nations Environment Programme (UNEP) estimated that there were 46,000 pieces of plastic litter per square mile of sea. And the rubbish isn't all far from home:

A total of 8,174 plastic bags were found on UK beaches during Beachwatch 2008 – that's 46.5 bags for every kilometer of beach surveyed.

Over 500 Combined Sewage Overflow pipes (CSOs) discharge sewage directly onto Britain's beaches. When there's too much water for the drain network to cope with it, as during a heavy storm, these pipes carry the extra sewage away, but many date to Victorian times and are no longer fit for purpose.

The Marine Conservation Society describes what is happening to our seas thus: 'too many fish are being taken out, too much rubbish is being thrown in, and too little is being done to protect our precious marine wildlife and vital fish stocks.'

Our seas and beaches should be a place for wildlife to thrive and people to enjoy. To ensure this, we need to campaign against corporate polluters and overfishing and to take individual responsibility for every piece of rubbish we throw away that may end up in the sea. If not, irreparable damage will be done to sea life and to coastal areas, so that we may be the last generation to ever enjoy a walk along a pristine sandy beach or snorkelling amongst the amazing fish found along a living coral reef.

Take Action

▶ *Send it back*. Surfers Against Sewage's Return to Offender campaign urges people who find litter washed up on beaches to send it back to the manufacturer, if identifiable. While it recognizes that the manufacturers didn't drop the litter themselves, it wants to encourage these businesses to improve their anti-littering messages, reduce their packaging, invest in low-impact packaging, and support grassroots anti-litter campaigns.

▶ *Adopt a beach*. Choose your favourite beach and 'adopt' it by registering with the Marine Conservation Society. As an adopter you'll help organize teams to clean up and survey litter found on the beach. Or if you don't want such a big commitment, join in on its annual Beachwatch Big Weekend, which takes place on the third weekend of September and involves a nationwide clean up of our beaches.

▶ *Hold on tightly*. Don't let go of helium-filled balloons – it seems like fun to watch them float away, but they float back down to earth and get mistaken for food by many sea creatures. Balloon plastics block these animals' digestive systems, causing them to starve.

Where to Get Started

With offices in the USA, UK, Australia, Switzerland, and Japan, the **Project AWARE Foundation** helps to conserve underwater environments through education, advocacy, and action programmes. In partnership with scuba divers and water enthusiasts, Project AWARE undertakes cleanups and coral reef conservation initiatives. It also monitors and collects data on marine environments and provides education programmes for children.
www.projectaware.org

Surfers Against Sewage (SAS) campaigns for safe recreational waters free from sewage effluents, toxic chemicals, marine litter, and nuclear waste.
Unit 2, Wheal Kitty Workshops
St Agnes
Cornwall TR5 0RD
Tel 01872 555 950
www.sas.org.uk

The **Marine Conservation Society** works to preserve and care for our seas, shores, and wildlife.
Unit 3, Wolf Business Park
Alton Road
Ross-on-Wye
Herefordshire HR9 5NB
Tel 01989 566 017
www.mcsuk.org

Number power: The impact of mass participation

Colin Butfield is Head of Campaigns at the environmental charity WWF UK (www.wwf.org.uk), the UK arm of the WWF Network, the world's leading environmental organization. Recent campaigns include What Wood You Choose?, highlighting illegal logging, and lobbying on behalf of the Marine and Coastal Access Act of 2009, which places a legal duty on the UK government to conserve and protect species and habitats in and around our seas.

Q *How can someone get started on a campaign?*

A A good way to start is by visiting the websites of some campaigning organizations. See if their issues are ones that really motivate you and if the way they campaign suits you. Often you can sign up to an e-newsletter which will tell you when campaigns are happening, and you can then decide what you want to get involved in.

Then pick an issue you really care about and see a campaign through with the organization. This way you get a feel of how a campaign runs and what different types of things you can do to support it; you get a real sense of being part of something. Sometimes when people are new to campaigning they get really excited, take loads and loads of different actions, then lose interest. But once you see something through and realize the power we all have to change things, you're in it for life!!

Q *Are mass events like stunts and marches important?*

A These are probably the best known campaign tactics and often the most fun, but they actually represent a pretty small part of most campaigns – and you certainly don't have to take part if it's not your thing. Most campaigns we run need a whole range of activities to make them work, from signing petitions to posting comments on a web page to writing to your MP to simply looking at a label before you buy a product.

Q *Are there other campaigning tools which can be used to demonstrate the numbers of people behind a cause?*

A There's no one answer to this. The most effective campaigns will always have spent a lot of time choosing the tools that are best suited to their issue. Some campaigns could involve getting as many people as possible to all do the same thing at the same time. For example, part of our climate change campaign involves an event called Earth Hour where we get millions of people and landmarks around the world to turn out their lights for an hour. Our campaigners will do things like host a candlelit dinner for their friends or get a local pub to run a themed evening.

Another useful tool is that of consumer power. We have a range of campaigns at the moment spanning our main themes of protecting the natural world, changing the way we live, and tackling climate change. Really big issues for us at the moment are deforestation and illegal logging, making the UK's homes, travel, and food supply sustainable, and campaigning across the world to tackle climate change. So we're trying to get our campaigners to spread the word about how to tell if a wood product – like garden furniture – is from a sustainable source or not.

43

Treat animals well

*The greatness of a nation and its moral progress can be
judged by the way its animals are treated*
MAHATMA GANDHI

It's not about whether you prefer cats to dogs or gerbils to hamsters, whether you eat animals or won't touch a boiled sweet if it's so much as looked a piece of gelatin in the eye. Nor is it about how cute an animal is or the companionship you get whilst walking your dog every day. How we treat animals is a reflection of how we are as human beings.

Animals need enough food, shelter, and stimulation to make being alive a pleasure, not a pain, for them – not for us. This means people breeding animals for food should provide minimum levels or care, people keeping animals as pets have a duty to treat them well, and every one of us should be aware of how to treat wild animals when we come across them.

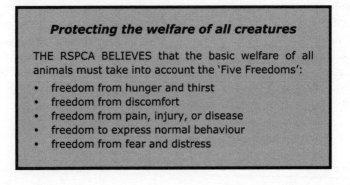

Protecting the welfare of all creatures

THE RSPCA BELIEVES that the basic welfare of all animals must take into account the 'Five Freedoms':

- freedom from hunger and thirst
- freedom from discomfort
- freedom from pain, injury, or disease
- freedom to express normal behaviour
- freedom from fear and distress

Simply put, understanding the importance of animal welfare stops us being animals ourselves.

Take Action

▶ *Report abuse*. If you see an animal being mistreated report it to the RSPCA or the police.

▶ *Be a responsible owner*. Ask your vet to embed a microchip with contact details in your pet, so if your pet gets lost you have more chance of being reunited. You can microchip cats, dogs, rabbits, and horses.

▶ *Offer a temporary home*. Fostering is possible for animals as well as children. There are some schemes to help give temporary homes to the pets of families fleeing domestic abuse until they get settled. Contact your local animal welfare charity for information about this and other rehousing programmes.

Where to Get Started

The **RSPCA** rescues animals, educates the public about animal welfare, and campaigns against animal cruelty.
Enquiries Service
Wilberforce Way
Southwater
Horsham
West Sussex RH13 9RS
RSPCA helpline to report animal cruelty 0300 1234 999
www.rspca.org.uk

Compassion in World Farming campaigns to end cruel factory-farming practices.
River Court
Mill Lane
Godalming
Surrey GU7 1EZ
Tel 01483 521 953
www.ciwf.org.uk

Purchase power:
Campaigning with your shopping basket

Mel Andrews is Campaign Manager at the RSPCA (www.rspca. org.uk), an animal welfare charity. One of its campaigns is Rooting for Pigs, which hopes to improve the living conditions of pigs bred for meat. Rather than urging people to give up their bacon butties, bangers and mash, or Sunday roast, the campaign asks people to think about the type of pork they eat.

Q *Tell me about your current campaign.*

A I'm running a campaign on farm animal welfare called Rooting for Pigs. We're lobbying to improve EU legislation that protects pig welfare. We're trying to educate consumers about the pork, bacon, and sausages that they buy, encouraging them to buy higher-welfare meat and to ask about the source of their meat when eating out in restaurants.

Q *Can this kind of small action really make a difference?*

A Even just changing your buying habits like this can be part of a campaign, when it comes to the environment or animal welfare.

Campaigning conjures up the image of waving a placard at a rally, but campaigning is so much more than this. Just telling a friend about where to buy more ethical products, or about a way to save energy, is campaigning. You can write a letter to your MP, forward a campaign email to a friend, set up a Facebook group, wear a T-shirt with a campaigning message on; the list is endless. There's something to suit everybody, whether you want to be on the TV making sure everyone has heard you, or you want to be behind the scenes helping to spread the word among friends.

Q *What campaigning tools do you think work best?*

A This really depends on what the issues are and what the campaign is trying to achieve. In some cases, the most effective way to get a campaign message across may be getting the support of a celebrity and holding a large public event. In other cases, it may be getting volunteers to go into their local communities and speak to individuals on a one-to-one basis. If you're trying to achieve political change, writing to your MP is an important step, and it's often better to write a letter than send an email. Social media has brought a whole new set of tools that enables campaigners to speak directly to thousands of people, with very little cost. Setting up a Facebook group, a Twitter account, an online petition, or a blog are all very effective ways of campaigning that you can fit in around your other life commitments.

Q *Can you give an example of a campaign you admire?*

A I really like the Fairtrade campaign (www.fairtrade.org.uk). It gives people easy steps of how they can help people in developing countries, just by changing what they buy. It has helped consumers to understand that just by making different choices in the supermarket, they can have a huge impact on the lives of people in other countries. It really shows the positive impact of making the right choices.

Q *What advice would you give people who want to get involved with campaigning, but don't know where to start?*

A Get involved and volunteer with charities that you believe in. Work on getting the skills that you need in areas such as communication, public relations, and marketing. There are some really easy online tools to help you set up a campaign, such as the website Louder (www.louder.org.uk). The site lets you set up a campaign, host a petition, encourage people to send a letter to their MP, and so on. It also lets you talk with other campaigners to get help and advice.

44

Appreciate art for art's sake

One of the key signs of a happy society is that its members produce and enjoy the arts. Not only does a vibrant arts scene show that we have the time and inclination to create things purely to make us think or to entertain ourselves, but it fosters free expression and inspires us. Exposure to the arts can also promote activity in the brain and provide a medium through which we communicate with one another. Through art we can make sense of the world around us, expressing our hopes and fears, and working through whatever questions or issues we may have.

Though the arts are often the first to suffer when it comes to government funding cuts, supporting the arts doesn't have to cost a lot of money. Arts Council England point out that funding to the tune of just 17p a week per person is all that it takes for the country to have an arts 'sector that gives Britain an international edge as a dynamic place to live, work, and do business; a sector which fuels the creative industries and generates future jobs in one of the fastest growing parts of the economy; and a sector with a proven track record of regenerating towns and cities and contributing to a cohesive and engaged society'. In fact, in 2007 the arts accounted for 2 million jobs and £16.6 billion of exports. The arts are also central to the UK's tourism industry, with several million visitors attending the theatre, ballet, opera, or concert during their visit.

From both a financial and emotional point of view, the arts are not an area we can afford to ignore.

Take Action

▶ *Look around you*. Take in the public art around you, from official statues in parks to street art murals. Then discuss it with your friends. You don't have to like it to appreciate its presence.

▶ *Visit galleries and museums*. Many public art venues are free, but they only remain free if they continue to get high visitor numbers and voluntary donations. When you visit, leave a donation if you can. If you're looking for a gift, consider buying something in a museum shop to help support its costs.

▶ *Bring art alive*. Many galleries and museums rely on volunteers to give talks or help visitors. Contact your favourite gallery and see what opportunities there are to get involved.

Where to Get Started

Arts Council England supports programmes to bring visual arts, literature, theatre, music, dance, and crafts to the general public. Scotland, Wales, and Northern Ireland also have equivalent bodies.
National Service Centre
The Hive
49 Lever Street
Manchester M1 1FN
Tel 0845 300 6200
www.artscouncil.org.uk

Organizing successful events:
The big picture and the small details

Jessica Studdert has been Events Director at an influential think tank and has worked for St Mungo's (www.mungos.org), the homelessness charity. Her top tips for organizing events cover thinking about what and who it involves, when and where it happens, why you're having the event, and how to follow up after the event.

What: the format

Do you want a small seminar with a group of experts to have a substantive discussion, get their buy-in as a key stakeholder, and give you in-depth feedback on your campaign and how to take it forward? Or do you want your event to have a broader audience, a wider discussion, and a higher profile to build momentum and open up the issue to a range of people?

A reception can be a useful way of gathering people together, but you'll only be able to get across topline information as people don't have a long attention span for speeches and they'll mostly be there for the networking. On the other hand, a discussion will get people more hooked in to the content and allow you to 'platform' your key messages well. A conference can be useful to cover a range of issues in one day, but this should be carefully structured to cover all bases, not be repetitive, and be genuinely useful for people to justify a day out of their time to attend.

Who: the speakers

Speakers should be strong advocates of your cause and able to make an eloquent case. You can invite people to speak that you want to influence – this is a good opportunity to get them engaged with your campaign's messages and also to hear what their position is, something that can help inform your own strategy as it develops. Speakers should be fun and engaging – and try to think outside the box. Some people are known for speaking on various issues, so try not to be predictable, as this will make for a more enjoyable event for those present. Can you call on people the campaign affects directly, that is, 'self advocates'?

When putting a panel together, don't always look for agreement. Try to mix things up by putting people up there who might bring different perspectives to the table and be able to have a good debate. This enthuses and engages people in the audience much more than a load of people agreeing with one another.

When: the timing

The timing of an event is crucial – it should be used as part of a wider campaign for maximum impact. It could be a launch to start the campaign, or a conclusion to present results or findings and take them forward. Think about what else is going on in the outside world that is relevant – could you hook onto another issue and get some momentum from that? Do you need to be aware of which days Parliamentarians are in London and which days they are in their constituencies and do you need to factor in the long recesses when they are away from Westminster? Do you need to consider press timings (that is, a press conference needs to be in the morning so that journalists have the rest of the day to follow up)?

Who: the attendees

Think about who needs to be there: Who are you trying to influence or involve? A diverse range of people from different professions, sectors, and backgrounds will make for a better discussion on the day, and serve to broaden your campaign's appeal in the longer term. Invite top-level people but be prepared for them to sometimes send a substitute.

Invite people in good time – send out an initial invite two months to six weeks in advance, then follow up with reminders nearer the time. Make sure it is clear where people need to send their RSVP.

Mail merge is a great invention. Use it to personalize invites, as people respond to a personal message much better than something that looks like a general round-robin.

How many: the attendees

Keep an eye on capacity – you should over-invite for a seminar by about three times the capacity, and for a broader event by about ten times the capacity. But remember that about a third of people who RSVP won't actually turn up on the day, so do over-accept RSVPs.

And remember a small packed room looks better than a big empty one, so have a target capacity and go for it – be prepared to downsize rooms if it's going to look too empty, or set out a smaller number of chairs close to the front of the room so that they are all taken and it still looks buzzy. There is nothing worse than an empty reception or room, it can make your campaign appear as though there's nothing behind it or no interest, so make sure you take measures to boost capacity – calling people who have RSVPed to check they are coming, sending out good directions and a reminder the day before, and being prepared to invite more people as you get nearer the day if you find yourself short on numbers as the date approaches.

Where: the venue

Make sure the venue suits your needs. Staff being helpful and courteous is really important, so take recommendations and go back to venues you've had a good experience with. Make sure the venue has disabled access, a hearing loop for people with hearing aids and disabled parking – attendees may ask questions about access and facilities that you need to be able to answer. The location is important – make it as easy as possible for people to come. It may be that you can think of a quirky venue that will underpin and reinforce your messages or campaign.

Catering

If you can, offer some food or drink – people like this and are much more likely to stay around before or after if you bribe them with treats.

On the day: setting clear roles

One main organizer should be responsible for allocating clear roles to people running the event. You could do a schedule, so that people know how things will run and when, but also clearly allocate people to different tasks, so that you can be confident things will run themselves on the day. Brief colleagues in advance. Make sure your speakers are well cared for. They have all taken the time to participate, and some can be rather self important. Treat them professionally and they will be more likely to remain engaged.

After the event: making it pay off

Before you have the event, you should have a clear idea of where it sits in the context of a wider campaign, who is coming, and what you want to achieve. It's no good having an event if you don't take the opportunity to capitalize on the occasion and the contacts you'll make. Have a clear idea in advance what you want out of people. Send a general thank-you note with some information (maybe a speech or a briefing of what was said) to all attendees, then follow up with individuals personally. Make sure you gather good contact details from people to enable you to do this, and try to see the event as a platform from which to build momentum and involvement.

Finally, make it fun!

People respond best to fun, useful, and interesting things. You might be opening their eyes to something for the first time, or putting out a new slant on something. Whatever the reason for your case, and even if it's professionals that need to be there because of their jobs, make sure the experience is fun and rewarding – the attendees will think more positively of you and your campaign, and it will serve to boost recognition of your work. There's no need for people to be bored into submission, make them laugh and they'll listen more attentively!

45

Increase literacy and basic skills

If you are reading this book, even if you don't agree with some of the issues it raises, you are fortunate. Being able to read and write opens up many opportunities for you. It means you can write job applications, send messages to friends and family, and entertain yourself with a book. But more than that, it means you can get by in life without relying on others to help – you can write a shopping list, read road signs, write a birthday card, understand a bill, flick through a newspaper, and so on.

According to the National Literacy Trust, one in six people in the UK struggle to read and write. People who are illiterate earn less, as fewer jobs are open to them, and they tend to have lower confidence and lower levels of happiness. For these reasons, ensuring people have the basic skills they need when it comes to reading and writing is one of the best ways to improve their well-being and livelihoods – that's how important it is.

Take Action

▶ *Join – and use – your local library.* Libraries are an amazing resource providing free books and information to everyone who needs them. But when library use goes down, libraries are easy targets for government budget cuts. If we don't use them, we'll lose them.

▶ *Read to people, and not just to children*. Reading can be a communal activity as well as a solitary pastime, and encourages everyone to develop their reading skills.

▶ *Fill the bookshelves*. You can buy books or donate your used copies to support literacy causes. Better World Books (www.betterworldbooks.co.uk) is a socially and environmentally responsible bookseller. It collects unwanted books and sells them online in support of various charities, including the National Literacy Trust. Those it can't sell it re-homes or recycles.

> *Reading is to the mind what exercise is to the body*
> JOSEPH ADDISON

Where to Get Started

The **National Literacy Trust** helps people in the UK to develop the reading, writing, speaking, and listening skills necessary for life.
68 South Lambeth Road
London SW8 1RL
www.literacytrust.org.uk

46

Use plain English

If information is written in jargon or goobledegook then it excludes many people from understanding it. In fact, using difficult words or complex sentences can be a deliberate smokescreen to stop people from asking questions or standing up for themselves, because if we don't understand something then our natural reaction is to fear it, mistrust it, or ignore it.

What's more, it is unreasonable to expect people to cope with their daily lives if they can't understand the information they are being given about it. This might be information about how to vote or about a benefit they are entitled to claim. In some cases it can even involve information affecting life and death, as shown by the Campaign for Plain English. It gathered case studies of people who have found some official forms so arduous that they have not filled them out, meaning they have not been able to claim for enough money to eat or to heat their houses.

Speaking and writing in plain English, particularly at an official level, is not about dumbing down language. It's about being concise and accurate and getting your message across in a way that as many people as possible can understand, in a language appropriate for your audience. Using plain English is the responsibility of anyone sending out a message.

Take Action

▶ *Send it back*. If you feel a form, leaflet, or information sheet is too difficult to understand, send it back to the originator and explain why. The Campaign for Plain English provides stickers you can put on it.

▶ *Don't be clever*. Encourage your employer to use plain English and always do so yourself. In the end, it's not clever at all to write something that people can't understand.

▶ *Make an example*. Send in examples of good and bad English to the Campaign for Plain English and similar organizations. You can even nominate entries for their annual awards.

Where to Get Started

The **Campaign for Plain English** fights against gobbledygook, jargon, and misleading public information in over eighty countries and awards crystal marks to organizations whose documents are written in plain English.
PO Box 3
New Mills
High Peak SK22 4QP
Tel 01663 744409
www.plainenglish.co.uk

The **Center for Plain Language** is a US-based organization working to ensure that government and business documents are clear and understandable.
3936 Rickover Road
Silver Spring, MD 20902
USA
Tel +1 301 219. 1731
www.centerforplainlanguage.org

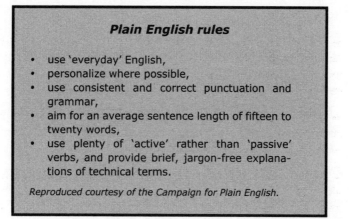

Plain English rules

- use 'everyday' English,
- personalize where possible,
- use consistent and correct punctuation and grammar,
- aim for an average sentence length of fifteen to twenty words,
- use plenty of 'active' rather than 'passive' verbs, and provide brief, jargon-free explanations of technical terms.

Reproduced courtesy of the Campaign for Plain English.

47

Support people with learning disabilities

The phrase 'learning disability' covers many conditions. What these conditions have in common is that people with a learning disability find it harder than normal to learn, understand, and communicate, often needing varying degrees of help with everyday tasks such as reading, eating, dressing, and going to the toilet. Sometimes, sadly, these difficulties are met with ridicule or discrimination.

The UK charity Mencap runs a number of programmes regarding fair treatment for people with learning disabilities. Its campaigns include better health provision, as people with a learning disability are more likely to have poor health or suffer from serious conditions; further, many healthcare professionals do not understand learning disability. Mencap also supports access to good-quality continuing education and job training.

Supporting people with a learning disability involves ensuring they can have fun like everyone else. Imagine being out at a gig or party and having to leave because your support worker's shift has finished. That lack of independence is what some people with a learning disability face.

A key part of living in a fair and tolerant society is the belief that all people should have the same rights and opportunities. This applies to people with learning disabilities as much as anyone else. Yet the 1.5 million people with a learning disability in the UK are often treated as second-class citizens – a state of affairs we need to end.

Take Action

▶ *Consider your treatment.* People with a learning disability can be at risk of bad treatment and hate crime. Make sure you treat people with a learning disability as you would like to be treated yourself, and speak out if you see someone with a learning disability being treated badly.

▶ *Create opportunities.* If you are an employer consider hiring someone with a learning disability. There is help and support available to do this. According to Mencap, 65 per cent of people with a learning disability want to work, but only one in ten people with a learning disability known to social services is in paid work. Help to make the difference.

Where to Get Started

Mencap supports people with a
learning disability, their families,
and their carers.
123 Golden Lane
London EC1Y 0RT
Tel 020 7454 0454
www.mencap.org.uk

'PEOPLE WITH A LEARNING DISABILITY don't get equal healthcare and thus experience worse outcomes. They receive fewer health screenings and are often treated by doctors and nurses who do not understand learning disability. Many have died prematurely. Mencap is campaigning to ensure people with a learning disability receive equal access to safe healthcare.

In 2007 Mencap launched a campaign called Death by Indifference. The "Death by Indifference" report contained evidence that people with a learning disability were dying unnecessarily due to institutional discrimination in the NHS. The report included six cases where people with a learning disability had died unnecessarily due to widespread ignorance and neglect within the NHS. As a result of our campaign and report the government ordered an independent inquiry to find out what was happening to people with a learning disability in the NHS. The Health Ombudsman also described these six cases in their "Six Lives" report. It criticized hospitals for failing to provide the proper level of care to people with a learning disability and highlighted an appalling catalogue of neglect and ignorance that led to these deaths.

After publishing the "Death by Indifference" report, Mencap received more accounts of tragic cases from families and carers. So we launched the Getting it Right campaign. This campaign seeks to improve healthcare for people with a learning disability. For it, Mencap has worked in partnership with a number of organizations, including Royal Colleges, to produce a charter for healthcare professionals to help them work towards better health, wellbeing, and quality of life for people with a learning disability. As of October 2010, ninety-three health authorities have signed the charter, including five out of ten Strategic Health Authorities.

As part of the campaign Mencap also commissioned a poll of healthcare professionals. This found that almost half of doctors (46 per cent) and a third of nurses (37 per cent) say that people with a learning disability receive a poorer standard of healthcare than the rest of the population. We launched the survey to the media alongside a number of case studies of people with a learning disability who had died unnecessarily in NHS hospitals, which led to lots of coverage in the press and on television and radio.

We also held marketing events throughout the UK where local campaigners took to the streets dressed in hospital scrubs and carrying placards to engage with the general public and to encourage them to sign on to our Getting it Right petition. The petition calls for a stop to people with a learning disability being denied equal healthcare. It currently has 7000 signatures. We intend to use this to show policy makers the strength of feeling there is over this issue.'

David Congdon, Head of Policy and Campaigns at Mencap

The official line:
Protesting against wrong decisions

Louise Wallis is Policy and Campaigns Officer at Respond (www.respond.org.uk), a charity that supports people with a learning disability who have been affected by abuse, sexual abuse, or hate crime. In 2010 Respond campaigned against Channel 4 and the broadcasting regulator Ofcom after celebrity Vinnie Jones and presenter Davina McCall made jokes about 'retards' on the TV show *Big Brother's Big Mouth* and Jones demonstrated a 'retard's walk'.

Q *Why was this so offensive?*

A Hate crime starts with verbal abuse. Words are important because they frame the way we see people. The word 'retard' derives from the medical term 'mental retardation'. It is important to challenge the derogatory use of the word 'retard' because it literally means 'a person with a learning disability'. When you say 'don't act like a retard', you are actually saying 'don't act like a person with a learning disability'. We have noticed the R-word is becoming more commonly used in the UK and, as it is always used in a derogatory way, we felt it was very important to challenge it.

Celebrities are role models and have considerable influence – increasingly so in today's celeb-obsessed culture. They need to remember that people with a learning disability are being harassed, abused, beaten, and even murdered because of their disability and that, sadly, people with a learning disability have a very low status in society. This leads to them being objectified and seen as inferior or even sub-human.

Q *What made you get involved with this campaign?*

A In early February 2010, Nicola Clark, the mother of two disabled daughters, contacted me to let me know that Vinnie Jones and Davina McCall had been joking about 'retards' on TV. I said Respond would like to run a campaign. I set up a Facebook group and registered complaints with Channel 4 and Ofcom. I emailed Channel 4's Disability Editor, too – she emailed me back the same day with a formal apology. But Ofcom wrote to me saying it had decided not to uphold my complaint.

Q *What was your response to Ofcom?*

A We decided to hold a protest at Ofcom on 3 March, as this was the official 'End the R-word Day'.

The main aim of the protest was to hand in a letter to Ofcom asking them to review their decision not to uphold viewers' complaints. We decided to ring Ofcom half an hour before we left, so that they knew we were coming; we wanted to make sure everyone taking part would be safe. Ofcom staff got into a bit of a panic as they hadn't had a protest before. About twenty of us got the bus to Ofcom's glass-fronted building in London. As we got there hundreds of Ofcom staff were at the windows to watch us. We held up our banners for them all to see. They said 'Ofcom the R-word is no joke', 'No to hate crime', and 'Mind your language'. Then we stood peacefully outside the building. Next Ofcom sent down on a senior manager to collect our letter. One of our protestors also treated him to a forthright lecture on the R-word. We stayed outside Ofcom for about an hour, holding our placards for passers-by.

Among the people with a learning disability who protested outside Ofcom were DJs and MCs from the Wild Bunch, a night club run by people with a learning disability (www.wildbunch-club.com). They had already done some campaign work on the R-word, so when they heard about the Vinnie Jones incident they were keen to protest.

Q *Were there any problems?*

A One of our members was busting to go to the toilet, so we asked the security guard if he'd let him in to use the loo. The poor guard didn't know what to do. He couldn't risk compromising the security of the building but there was also a disabled man with his legs crossed needing to go. Compassion won the day and our guy and his support worker were allowed in.

Q *Did the protest succeed?*

A Later that month the charity Mencap published research show-ing that viewers do consider the R-word to be offensive and launched an e-campaign encouraging supporters to email Ofcom's chief executive. On 27 April 2010 Ofcom's Broadcasting Review Committee met to reconsider the case, and on the same day Jackie Ryan (one of the people with learning difficulties who took part in the Ofcom protest) appeared on the Radio 4 pro-gramme *Word of Mouth* talking about the R-word.

In May Ofcom announced it had changed its decision: Channel 4 was found to have breached the Broadcasting Code and our complaint was upheld. This ruling has had major implications for all broadcasters, who are now finally required to take this kind of discrimination as seriously as racism.

48

Educate everyone

Education is the most powerful weapon which you can use to change the world
NELSON MANDELA

The idea of education for all has many facets to it. In the UK it is about ensuring people with special needs have the help and support they need to get a good education and that all schools and educational establishments have the resources and staff needed to ensure high standards across the board.

Elsewhere in the world the campaign for universal education is often about ensuring that schools and teachers exist and that children are able to attend school even if their families live in extreme poverty and they are needed to work. And in some parts of the world it's about ensuring girls have the same access to education as boys. According to Oxfam, 72 million children in the developing world do not get a school education. To help change this, 2 million new teachers are needed.

Because not only should education be an end in itself, helping people to get the most out of life, but the skills learnt in school, particularly reading and writing, are the very skills that help people to escape from poverty.

Take Action

▶ *If you can, teach.* If you are a qualified teacher, consider spending some time working abroad through VSO (www.vso.org.uk), an international development organization that enlists volunteers to fight poverty in developing countries.

▶ *Find a twin.* If you are at school, or work or have children at a local school, see whether your school can pair up with a school in a developing country and swap information about your lives. This can happen by letter or, if both schools have computers, online. Your school could also fundraise to help its twin school.

▶ *Donate knowledge.* Some charities will recycle books and other educational resources and send them to schools in developing countries that need them. An internet search will help you find those that do this, or to make contact with schools yourself and see whether they would welcome you arranging this independently.

Where to Get Started

The **Global Campaign for Education** (GCE) seeks to ensure that governments deliver the right of every girl, boy, woman, and man to a free, quality public education.
PO Box 521733
Saxonwold
Johannesburg 2132
South Africa
Tel +27 (0)11 447 4111
www.campaignforeducation.org

Global Gateway is a resource for local schools interested in partnering with a school elsewhere in the world.
Tel 0161 957 7755
www.globalgateway.org

49

Prepare for disasters and respond quickly to emergencies

In the past few years many natural disasters have shocked the world, from floods to tsunamis, hurricanes to earthquakes, volcanoes to famine.

There's not a lot we can do to stop many of these disasters from happening, but we can try to ensure infrastructure on the ground is as strong as possible to prevent some of the worst damage. According to the British Red Cross, every £1 invested in reducing the threat of a disaster saves £4 in emergency response and reconstruction. Such prevention requires ensuring local people in areas prone to natural disasters have in place the skills and resources to respond to emergencies, including life-saving equipment, food, blankets, and hygiene kits. It also requires vigilance in anticipating human-made disasters, since these preparations can be thwarted by conflict, bad governance, or poor infrastructure.

When a disaster does happen, we also need to help by giving money for much needed immediate aid – and to not fall prey to 'disaster fatigue'. For example, an appeal by the Disasters Emergency Committee (DEC) after the January 2010 Haiti Earthquake raised over £100 million from the UK, but it took weeks to get public attention for the Pakistan floods later in the year.

Take Action

▶ *Support development*. Not all politicians make overseas development a priority, and having long-term aid allows countries to build the infrastructure for responding to disasters. The Department of International Development was started in 1997 'to promote sustainable development and eliminate world poverty'. Keep pressure on government, whichever party is in charge, to ensure this department continues with appropriate funding.

▶ *Give generously*. Donate to organizations helping developing countries before a disaster happens, and donate to relief efforts in the aftermath of one.

▶ *Volunteer*. If you would like to volunteer in the humanitarian field, have a look at the courses offered by RedR UK (www.redr.org.uk). If its training is for you, sign up. Afterwards, the VSO (www.vso.org.uk) have a range of placements around the world for people of all ages with many different skill types.

Where to Get Started

The **Disasters Emergency Committee** (DEC) is an umbrella organization for thirteen humanitarian aid agencies. When an emergency happens, DEC brings these organizations together to raise funds and ensure the funds go to the agencies best placed to deliver relief to the people most in need.
First Floor, 43 Chalton Street
London NW1 1DU
Tel 020 7387 0200
www.dec.org.uk

The **British Red Cross** responds to disasters in the UK and around the world. It also helps communities to be prepared in case of a disaster.
44 Moorfields
London EC2Y 9AL
Tel 0844 871 1111
www.redcross.org.uk

Think local:
When your councillor can help

Luke Akehurst has been a Labour Party Councillor for Chatham Ward in the London Borough of Hackney since 2002. The main issues facing his ward are social housing, crime and anti-social behaviour, and health issues connected to deprivation, and issues he's campaigned on include winning funding for new security doors on local estates and bringing in parking controls.

Q *What issues can people contact their councillor about?*

A Any issue that relates to the responsibilities of the council. In a unitary council such as a London Borough this could include housing, crime, and anti-social behaviour prevention, schools and nurseries, social care, public health, the local environment, parks, libraries, leisure centres, waste management and recycling, community cohesion, and the 'general wellbeing' of the area. Generally councillors will refer issues that are purely national to the local MP or parliamentary candidate, and vice versa.

Q *What makes you likely to take people seriously if they approach you about an issue?*

A If they can demonstrate it affects residents of my ward, and if they have a defined objective that it is realistic to achieve. Basically I will get heavily stuck in to an issue if it's something where I have a chance of getting a result through the council's policy making structures.

Q *What can you do to help people?*

A As a councillor I can be a voice and an advocate who can shout for them when the council's executive takes decisions. I can write letters, lobby the leader or mayor or senior council officers, table motions, or bring petitions or deputations to full council. Often I'll be able to suggest ways forward or sources of funding that members of the public might not be aware of.

Q *Who can't you help?*

A You can't be on two sides of the argument – for instance, I had some local residents who wanted controlled parking introduced and some who didn't. I had to make a decision about which side of the debate I was on, based on the weight of local opinion and my own political judgement about the merits of the policy.

Q *Can you give an example of a successful campaign you've been involved with?*

A I campaigned to get a local road 'adopted' – it was technically a private road and had been since the 1920s, so the road surface and pavements were unmaintained and there was no street lighting. Initially council officers said it was too expensive for it to become a public road and the responsibility of the council, but I kept pushing with the Residents' Association and now it is properly maintained and lit.

Q *Any tips for people who care strongly about an issue and want to start campaigning on it?*

A Go to your councillor and get him or her onside at the start of planning a campaign, not right at the end. Often quiet diplomacy behind the scenes by a councillor is more effective than grandstanding with motions and deputations to council or coverage in the local paper.

50

Use your vote

In the 2010 UK General Election, voter turnout stood at 65.1 per cent. Although this was high compared to recent elections (it was 59.4 per cent in 2001), it still means that 34.9 per cent of eligible voters didn't turn up at the polls. If each of the people who could vote but didn't had used his or her vote, the election result could have been very different.

It's not just that people wait until the day of the election and then decide they are too busy to make it to the polling station or realize they can't decide who to vote for. In early 2010, just months before the election was held, the Electoral Commission found that more than half of young people eligible to vote were not registered to do so.

One favourite argument is that all politicians are the same – the only difference is the colour of their party logo. But compare their policies, voting records, and speeches and you will see that argument just doesn't wash. Politicians hold a range of very different core ideologies, from believing in a safety net of welfare for anyone who needs it to a survival-of-the-fittest mentality that puts an unbridled market ahead of the economically vulnerable; and from inclusive outlooks to racist mentalities that classify many people as second-class citizens – or not as citizens at all.

We don't hesitate to complain about our elected representatives at all levels if we don't like the decisions they make, so why are so many people so hesitant about using one of the best tools they have at their disposal to change who's sitting in office?

Take Action

▶ *Sign up*. Register to vote, and then use your vote at election time. If you don't know which person you support then go to local hustings where candidates speak about their beliefs, and read the manifestos where parties spell out the policies they would like to enact if they win.

▶ *Find out*. Learn how the voting system works and about the types of representatives there are. If you don't understand how the system works you will never be able to change it.

▶ *Put yourself forward*. If you don't like any of the candidates available for your vote, think about standing for election yourself. Independents can and do win elections; however, you're more likely to find success with party backing, so read literature on the websites of the political parties and work out which one best suits your beliefs.

▶ *Be persuasive*. Convince your friends and family to vote, and talk to them about the issues you feel are important.

Registering to vote

EACH YEAR BETWEEN August and November, local Electoral Registration Offices deliver registration forms to every home in the country in what is known as the 'annual canvass'. This allows you to register to vote by returning the form to the address given. At other times of the year you can download a form from the Electoral Commission website and register to vote.

To find out whether you are on the electoral register call your local council, which should be able to check for you.

Where to Get Started

In addition to administering elections, the **Electoral Commission** offers advice on standing for election, registering a political party, and deciphering election rules. The commission has offices serving Northern Ireland, Scotland, and Wales, as well as four regional offices in England.
Trevelyan House
Great Peter Street
London SW1P 2HW
Tel 020 7271 0500
www.electoralcommission.org.uk

51

Care about climate change

Climate change is a massive issue. It's a catch-all term that refers to changes in the earth's temperature as a result of human behaviour and their consequences, such as rising sea levels and extreme weather conditions.

But although most of us recognize the importance of caring about climate change, for many of us the enormity of the problem seems to make it too big to do anything about. Does it make a difference to reduce your own carbon footprint, or do you need to be lobbying politicians to change the way the whole world uses energy?

The following organizations provide a wealth of information about climate change and the actions you can take to try to slow it down or stop it:

Climate Concern UK (www.climate-concern.com)
Friends of the Earth (www.foe.org.uk)
Greenpeace (www.greenpeace.org.uk)
Oxfam (www.oxfam.org.uk)
Stop Climate Chaos Coalition (www.stopclimatechaos.org)
WWF (www.wwf.org.uk)

Afterword:
What are you going to shout about?

Throughout this book I've provided a range of issues that I believe are worth campaigning about, and a range of actions to help you do something about them. Some of these actions require one click of a computer mouse, others require making a change in your daily habits, still others require a significant investment of time and expertise. Hopefully at least a few of them will capture your imagination and make you think 'I'm going to do that', because just a little bit of your time, a public declaration of what you believe to be right or wrong, or a small action can be the catalyst for things to change in order to make your community, your country, and even the world a little bit nicer.

What are you going to shout about?

When ... to get started	Who ... I'm campaigning for	What ... my commitment to action is	How ... to 'make it local'	Why ... it's important to me
This week				
In the next month				
In the next six months				
In the next year				

Acknowledgements

Many people and organizations have been incredibly generous with their knowledge, contacts, and experience to enable me to write this book, or have provided invaluable information on their websites and in their publications and I would like to thank them.

For specific contributions and interviews: Richard Messingham (my husband and also a contributor to two sections of this book) and Adrian Lovett, Andrew Neilson, Annu Mayor, Clare White, Colin Butfield, David Russell, David Congdon, Elaine Londesborough-van Rooyen, Emily Kelly, Emily Thornberry, Gary Nunn, Geraldine Holden, Jessica Asato, Jessica Studdert, Kate Groucutt, Kathy Voss, Keiron Pim, Kerry McCarthy, Kirstie Hayward, Kristen Lindop, Louise Elliott, Louise Wallis, Lucy Lloyd-Ruck, Luke Akehurst , Malcolm Clark, Marie Clair, Mark Day, Megan Pacey, Mel Andrews, Michelle Smith, Patricia Hollis, Paul Eagle, Richard Lane, Sam Bacon, Stephanie Robertson, Wes Streeting, and William Perrin.

For other help and information: Anna Lindsay, Beth Breeze, Che Bishop, Clare Morgan, Conor McGinn, Domino Albert, Ellen Hewings, Hannah Smith, Hugo Manassei, James Harris, James Savage, Jo Cartwright, Jo Pratt, Judith Higgin, Katie Brewin, Neil Martin, Richard Simcox, Robin Hewings, Ruth Attride, and Vicky Trimikliniotis.

And: Abortion Rights, Age UK, American Civil Liberties Union, Amnesty International, Arts Council England, Avert, Better Banking Campaign, Brook, British Heart Foundation,

British Red Cross, Campaign for Plain English, Cancer Research UK, Carers UK, Center for the Victims of Torture, Contact the Elderly, Citizenship Foundation, Crisis, Dignity in Dying, Disability Sport Events, Disasters Emergency Committee, Electoral Commission, End Hunger Network, Equality and Human Rights Commission, Equality Trust, Fairtrade Foundation, Fight for Sight, FPA, Friends of the Earth, Bill and Melinda Gates Foundation, Help the Hospices, Howard League for Penal Reform, Innocence Project, London Citizens, Love Food Hate Waste, Marine Conservation Society, Mencap, Mental Health Foundation, Mumsnet, Nacro, National AIDS Trust, National Coalition to Abolish the Death Penalty, National Literacy Trust, OneWorld Network, Oxfam, Parentline Plus, PCS, Prison Reform Trust, Project Aware, Rainforest Foundation UK, Refugee Council, Reporters Without Borders, Respond, Rethink, Royal British Legion, RSPCA, Save the Children, Serious Organised Crime Agency, Shelter, St Mungo's, Stonewall, Stop Hate UK, Surfers Against Sewage , Survival International, Survivor's Fund, Sustrans, Talk About Local, Terrence Higgins Trust, Time to Change, Trades Union Congress, Unicef, WaterAid, World Health Organization, WWF, Young People's Trust for the Environment, Veterans of Foreign Wars of the United States, YouthNet UK, and YoungMinds.

Thanks also to Marsha Filion at Oneworld for her initial enthusiasm about the idea, Jonathan Conway, my agent, for his ongoing help and support, and Robin Dennis who edited this book for her encouragement, editing skills, and input. And an extra thanks to Helen Dalton and Helen Thorpe for their work on this book as interns at Oneworld.

Index